THE PEGGED JOINT

RESTORING ARTS & CRAFTS FURNITURE AND FINISHES

BY
BRUCE JOHNSON

Readers are urged to consider every restoration and refinishing product to be potentially harmful if not handled and stored properly. Read and follow all precautions and procedures according to the manufacturer's instructions. Wear the proper safety equipment, including protective glasses, gloves, and respirator. Provide adequate ventilation in your work area. Place rags and waste immediately after use in a sealed, water-filled metal container. Dispose of in accordance with local regulations.

Copyright © 1995 by Bruce E. Johnson

All rights reserved.
First Printing, February 1995
Published and distributed by
Knock On Wood Publications
A division of Wood-Care, Inc.
P.O. Box 8773
Asheville, NC 28814

ISBN: 1-886840-00-8
Library of Congress Catalog Number: 94-096788

TABLE OF CONTENTS

Introduction   4.

A Little Journey to an
       Arts & Crafts Workshop   7.

Setting Up an Arts & Crafts Workshop   17.

Identifying an Original Finish   25.

Finding and Protecting Shopmarks   31.

Making Repairs   37.

Wood Preparation   45.
       Stripping   46.
       Sanding   50.

Arts & Crafts Colors   53.
       Fuming   55.
       Aniline Dyes   61.
       Chemical Stains   64.
       Oil-based Stains   65.
       Paste Filler   67.

Arts & Crafts Finishes 71.
       Shellac   72.
       Varnish   77.
       Wax   82.
       Rubbing Out   86.

Maintaining Arts & Crafts Furniture   89.

Sources of Materials   93.

INTRODUCTION
4.

Though we generally associate the rediscovery of the Arts & Crafts movement with the 1972 Princeton exhibition, *The Arts & Crafts Movement in America*, an appreciation for Arts & Crafts finishes developed more slowly. For many years collectors had assumed the dark finishes on much of their Stickley, Roycroft, and Limbert furniture had resulted from years of toil and age. Only after many original finishes had been stripped and replaced with lighter stains and finishes did researchers discover that many Arts & Crafts furniture manufacturers had purposely fumed, dyed, and tinted their furniture dark tones of red, brown, and black. Now we realize original finishes are as important to our Arts & Crafts antiques as keyed tenons and leather tops.

When you also consider the number of pieces which have been painted, pushed outdoors, or sanded down to golden oak, we are fortunate to have as many original examples as we do to study. Given our new understanding and appreciation, collectors want to be able to preserve those finishes which have survived — and to duplicate those which have been destroyed.

Preserving, restoring, or duplicating an Arts & Crafts finish, however, is not as simple as opening a can with a screwdriver. Many Arts & Crafts manufacturers cloaked their formulas in mystery to prevent their competitors from duplicating the colors and finishes they had worked years to perfect. And to complicate matters, formulas and techniques which worked on new oak in 1905 do not always produce the same results on wood which is now ninety years old.

To further complicate matters, Gustav Stickley and Charles Limbert did not have to consider the proper way to repair Arts & Crafts furniture or to restore a finish which had experienced nearly nine decades of use and abuse. Their goals were to build furniture which would last and to protect it with a finish which would compliment both the wood they had selected and the design they had created. Our challenge is not only to be able to duplicate their finishes, but to restore and preserve the original finishes which have survived.

Our first responsibility should always be to the antique, for in truth we are borrowers rather than owners. Our personal preferences should never dominate historical accuracy. We have to recognize our own limitations, promising never to experiment on a valuable antique. Repairs and restoration beyond our abilities should be turned over to trusted, experienced professionals. When in doubt, hesitate. Do more research, ask more questions, conduct more experiments on scrap wood. Don't use a fine and rare antique as your laboratory experiment. The level of your expertise must surpass that of the value of the antique.

This treatise on Arts & Crafts furniture and their finishes has evolved over twenty-five years of study, enjoyment, and experience. More recently, when I made the decision to write this book, I attempted to read and decipher as much as I could find on the furniture stains and finishes prevalent during the first quarter of the twentieth century.

What I have discovered in my research and as a student of Arts & Crafts furniture has led me to believe that while there were many variations of Arts & Crafts stains and finishes, the ordinary collectors — given the proper instructions and materials — can easily preserve, restore, and duplicate an Arts & Crafts finish.

Als ik kan

Bruce Johnson
Asheville, North Carolina

A LITTLE JOURNEY TO AN ARTS & CRAFTS WORKSHOP

7.

While 19th-century manufacturers of Victorian furniture tended to remain anonymous, preferring to leave the advertising, promotion, marketing, and even the marking of their furniture to retail store owners, Arts & Crafts furniture makers took a decidedly different approach. For the first time in furniture history an entire group of manufacturers took it upon themselves to affix to their furniture a unique mark — be it a metal tag, paper label, brand, stamp, or decal — which identified their firm.

Many of these same firms also published catalogs illustrating individual pieces or room settings. In the introductions they would go to great lengths to distinguish their furniture from that of their competitors, describing the factory setting, the skills of their workers, the materials and construction techniques, and the finishes they applied.

Although most firms stopped short of providing the readers and their competitors with detailed formulas, the catalog introductions do provide a glimpse into Arts & Crafts workshops and the finishes they had developed. Realizing, of course, that manufacturers continued to modify and improve their finishes before, during, and after publication of any catalog, we can distill from their words vital information.

GUSTAV STICKLEY

— from Craftsman Homes (1909)

"This is a case where art must come to the aid of nature, because to leave the wood in the purely natural state would be to leave it exposed to all manner of soil and stain from wear. Also, the natural color of new oak is rather uninteresting; it needs age and exposure to give it the depth and mellowness which we associate with this wood. So, while our whole object is to keep the wood looking entirely natural in its possession of all the qualities which belong to oak, this can be done by the most careful treatment.

"Some time ago it was discovered that the fumes of ammonia would, within a very short time, darken white oak naturally, giving it the appearance which ordinarily would result from age and use. Therefore, as soon as a piece of Craftsman furniture is made, it is first moistened all over to open the pores, and then is put into an airtight compartment, on the floor of which are placed basins of very strong (26%) ammonia. The time usually demanded for this fuming is forty-eight hours, but that is varied according to the wood and the depth of color required. After the fuming the wood is carefully sand papered by hand until all the loose fibre is rubbed away and every trace of roughness removed.

"Then comes the final finish. For years I worked and experimented to find something that would leave the furniture entirely free from the hard glaze given by the use of shellac or varnish and yet would completely protect it not only from soil or stain but also from the atmospheric changes which cause it to shrink or swell. It was a difficult problem, — that of finding a method of finishing which would preserve all the woody quality of the oak without sacrificing the protection needed to make it "stand" under widely varying climatic conditions, — and it is only recently [ca. 1909] that I hit upon a solution which satisfies me.

"I found that all that is required to develop the best qualities of oak is to so ripen and mellow the wood that the full value of the natural color is brought out, as well as the individual beauty of texture and grain. The final finish we give it adds very little color, as our aim is rather to develop than to alter the natural tone of the wood, which always appears as an undertone under the surface tint.

"By the use of this finish we give the oak three different tones, all of which belong essentially to the wood. One is a light soft brown that is not unlike the hue of the frostbitten oak leaf; another is the rich nut brown tone which time gives to very old oak; and the third is a delicate gray that gives to the brown of the wood a silvery sheen such as might be produced by the action of the sun and wind.

"For the last rubbing we use the "Craftsman Wood Luster," which is not a varnish or a polish, but which gives a soft satiny lustre to the surface of the wood. When that surface is worn or soiled with use it may be fully restored — if the soil does not penetrate beyond the surface — by wiping if off with a piece of cheesecloth dampened with the Wood Luster and then rubbing it dry with a fresh cloth."

CHARLES LIMBERT

"In contrast to the high gloss and easily produced varnish finishes, Limbert's Holland Dutch Arts & Crafts finishes depend solely upon that soft, velvety, restful sheen and translucent color for their main charm, and for this reason, as may be well stated here, a finisher must be a man of vast experience and varied abilities, and let it be understood before going any further, the man who finishes our Holland Dutch Arts & Crafts furniture is worthy of a more dignified name than "finisher," for he must really be an artist and a chemist.

"A finisher must have an artist's taste and unerring eye for color and color harmony, and a chemist's knowledge of acids contained in different woods, and the effect of various chemicals upon these acids, to enable him to accentuate the natural beauties of the woods and bring out the latent grain markings through clear, transparent colors.

"Limbert's Holland Dutch Arts & Crafts furniture can be finished any special finish that can be made on White Oak, such as genuine Fumed, Flanders, Holland Oak, Weathered Early English, Stratford Oak, Golden Oak, Waxed, etc. or stained to match interior wood work or to harmonize with decorations, or furnished unfinished in the white.

"Genuine Fumed is the most popular finish for Arts and Crafts furniture. Our No. 8, autumn leaf brown, is the nut brown shade of Oak colored by age and use, and will harmonize with almost any color scheme. It is produced by placing White Oak, which contains tannic acid, in airtight boxes, and bringing it in contact with strong ammonia fumes for a number of days, until the fumes have thoroughly penetrated through the pores of the wood, and come in contact with the tannic acid, when a chemical change takes effect and discolors the wood through and through.

"After the furniture made of this wood is finished by our special process and waxed, a finish has been produced which is at once clear, translucent and smooth. This color will never wear off or show white on the edges or corners, as the wood is thoroughly impregnated with the ammonia fumes. Limbert's fuming process imparts to the surface a lustrous, iridescent life and glow and a warm, velvety sheen which cannot be produced with pigment stains applied with a brush, or any other method."

L. & J. G. STICKLEY

— ca. 1912 catalog

"The question of harmonizing color and finish is developed in the L. & J. G. Stickley Shops. And in this field of endeavor Leopold Stickley, "L" of the firm, one of the well known family of master workers in wood, has through several years of study and experiment arrived at expert knowledge of possible colors and undertones, treating the oak through fuming and staining, producing beauty of color as rich and glowing as that found on certain old canvasses.

"We appreciate the importance of harmonious color in the modern home and in the years devoted to making Handcraft we have given special attention to the preparation of stains and finishes. Our experiments have resulted in a treatment of oak that brings out its beauties of grain and texture and gives it soft dull tones of nut brown or of forest green. The furniture is subjected in airtight compartments to the fumes of strong ammonia, which penetrate and color the wood. It is then scraped and sanded, and is further treated with our stains and wax finishes until a smooth, satiny surface is obtained, delightful to touch and permanent in color."

"In reference to the #2 fumed oak finish, of course all of our #2 has always been fumed, and has to be in order to get this color; beyond this we use a #2 stain which we make ourselves and a colored shellac which we shade up with. It is a question in my mind if you have anyone who can lay on the colored shellac. We can furnish this if you so desire, however. You might possibly be able to spray the shellac on if you have an air gun."

— from a letter dated March 3, 1926 from L. & J.G. Stickley, Inc. to J.M. Young's Sons (provided by author Michael Clark)

STICKLEY BROTHERS

— from a 1902 catalog

"The wood most suited to this style, for the heavier work such as is required for halls, libraries and dens, is oak, with fumed wax finish (used so extensively in England during the past few years), which gives a beautiful delicate greyish-brown tone that cannot be obtained with any other finish. It also renders the wood most durable because the ammonia fumes which are employed penetrate deeply below the surface...."

In 1908 an ad appeared in the Grand Rapids *Furniture Record* for "Stickley's Quaint Brand Mission Finishes," including:

"**Stickley's Mission Stains** in all colors, very penetrating, can be either dipped or brushed, drying quickly and uniformly.

Stickley's Mission Wax in black and white, applies easily, drys to polish in thirty minutes, twenty-five per cent less waste than ordinary beeswax.

Stickley's Rapid-Lac the modern coating for quick effective work.

Stickley's Varnish Remover for use in removing old finishes, is the easiest, quickest and most economical on the market.

Also Mission Thinner, Mission Coating for interior and exterior, Klean-O for floors, Furniture Polish, etc."

THE ROYCROFT FURNITURE SHOP

— from a letter by Elbert Hubbard II, August 4, 1905

"None of our furniture has any varnish on it and doubtless the atmosphere [humidity] would not be taken into the wood so much were the stuff varnished. If we used varnish we would not be able to produce the particular weathered oak finish that we make and I think the color and texture of the finish are about the best I have ever seen. We are adopting a plan of shellacing all of the table tops and for that matter any pieces where three or four boards are joined together; I think that this will prevent to a great degree the swelling process that has been going on of late. You see the wood only swells sidewise and the dampness is all taken in on the end grain, swelling the ends of the boards first and opening the joints in the middle."

— from David Cathers' book

"Roycroft ads referred to their furniture's oak finish as a "weathered" finish, a combination of stain, filler, and wax polish. The actual formula of the finish was kept secret and apparently remains so to this day. However, Mr. Gerald Youngers, who had joined the furniture shop as an apprentice in 1913, shed some light on the nature of the formula in an interview with the author in 1979. Mr. Youngers said that the essence of the secret formula was a barrel of soupy water left standing, apparently for years on end, full of rusting nails and other pieces of scrap metal, and wood stain. This bizarre mixture was applied to the furniture by brush and left to stand. After it had completely dried and achieved a uniform overall color, the furniture was sanded to smooth the grain which had been raised by the watery stain. Wood filler was applied next, to fill in the open-pored oak, and then the furniture was waxed. The Roycroft finish gave a beautiful color to the wood, but it was not as durable as Stickley's shellac finish."

BRUSH, RAG OR SPRAYER?

Prior to the American Arts & Crafts movement, all furniture finishes were applied with either a brush or cloth. By 1900, however, most major furniture factories had electricity, opening the doors to table saws, planers, shapers, sanders, and spray equipment. Power machinery appears to have been more widely accepted more rapidly than equipment designed for spraying finishes. Insight into the acceptance by furniture manufacturers of spray equipment is provided by an article in the February 22, 1917 issue of *Furniture World* magazine:

> Furniture manufacturers will be interested in the statement that the Eureka Pneumatic Spray Co., of New York City, is the originator of the spraying system for finishing furniture. Its sprayers were the first on the market, dating back to the early part of 1900. Today these sprayers are extensively used all over the world for applying lacquer, paint, japan, enamel, shellac, varnish, bronze, etc., at an immeasurable advantage in cost over the old fashioned brush finishing and producing a superior result. Although on the market nearly seventeen years, it is only of comparatively recent date that sprayers have been used for furniture finishing. There appears to be two very good reasons for the delay in adopting this system on the part of the furniture manufacturing trade.
>
> First, because the varnish manufacturers did not try to make their product so that it could be sprayed to the best advantage. Second, because the expansion of the necessary air through a discharge orifice on the sprayer created cold, which chilled the varnish, causing the varnish to surface in a leathery or undulated surface. The Eureka Pneumatic Spray Co. met and overcame the second condition with its electric air heater.
>
> There is no longer any reason why manufacturers of furniture and other wood products should not now do their shellacking, varnishing, painting and enameling by the compressed air process with an air brush or sprayer. It means that a perfectly uniform surface will be obtained, doing away with nearly all of the sandpapering as well as rubbing. Spray finished work is not only produced at a savings of from 50%-80% in labor, but makes a substantial saving in the rubbing and sanding department.[1]

No information has yet surfaced which would indicate that Gustav Stickley, Charles Limbert, Stickley Brothers, the Roycrofters, or L. & J.G. Stickley utilized spray finish equipment on their Arts & Crafts furniture. In 1906, in fact, Gustav Stickley described the finish system at the Craftsman Workshops as follows:

> "After the desired color has been obtained, the surface of the wood is made satin-smooth by repeated applications of a specially prepared liquid finish, each coat being rubbed in with a piece of cloth."

While shellac and varnish can be applied using modern spray equipment, research indicates that it would not be required to duplicate an original Arts & Crafts finish.

1. Provided by Michael Clark and Jill-Thomas Clark, authors of J.M. Young Furniture, Dover Publications, 1994.

IS IT A RAG OR A CLOTH?

Generally speaking, any discarded material qualifies as a rag, regardless of its fibers. Synthetic fibers, though, do not absorb liquids as well as cotton; polyesters tend to smear liquids rather than absorbing them. Old cotton tee shirts and terrycloth towels work well for removing old finishes, but we don't always have a steady supply of them. Instead, you may have to buy packaged rags at your hardware store. While common rags may be suitable for wiping stripper off wood, they are not the best cloth for applying a finish, for even new rags tend to leave lint, dust, and loose fibers in the finish.

The best cloth applicators are made from new cheesecloth, a loosely-woven cloth made of 100% cotton fibers. Cheesecloth is available in either squares or lengths which you can cut to the desired size. Pound for pound, cheesecloth costs more than rags, but it far surpasses all competitors when it comes to applying a stain, dye, or finish.

WHAT KIND OF BRUSH?

Rather than arguing whether a synthetic bristle brush is superior to a natural bristle brush, I have discovered that all brushes actually fall into one of three different categories: cheap, moderately priced, and expensive. And I have also discovered that a better quality brush, regardless of its bristles, will lay down a smoother coat of finish.

When selecting a brush, look for one with flagged tips (they look like split ends), tapered bristles, good spring, and a tight metal ferrule (the band that attaches the bristles to the handle). Brush the bristles across the palm of your hand, checking to see how many come loose. Loose bristles are a trademark of an inexpensive brush — and can make your project look just as cheap.

The handle's length, diameter, shape, and material are personal choices and have no affect on the finish. It helps to have a brush which fits comfortably in your hand, but given the short amount of time you will be using it, the parts at the business end of the brush are more important.

Cheap foam brushes are only good for applying stains, for the air in the foam leaves bubbles in the finish. I use inexpensive bristle brushes (under $3) for applying stripper and stains; I buy moderately expensive brushes ($3-$6) for most of my finish work. And I have one or two expensive brushes ($7-$15) which are reserved exclusively for the final coat of my most important projects. I clean and reuse my finish brushes, but when they eventually degrade I reassign them to staining and stripping.

When shopping for brushes, remember this: using a cheap brush on a valuable antique is as satisfying as eating a fine meal with a plastic fork.

> **TIP:** When using a water-based stain, dye, chemical, or finish, use a synthetic bristle brush. Natural bristles absorb water and swell into uncontrollable blobs.

SETTING UP AN ARTS & CRAFTS WORKSHOP
17.

Unlike the wood worker, the wood finisher only needs a few basic tools to restore Arts & Crafts furniture. Some of the stains, dyes, and finish materials, however, are unavailable at local hardware and paint stores. Ordering small quantities of aniline dyes or tannic acid crystals before you need them can save you weeks of waiting later. Before buying any of the recommended tools and materials, read through the remainder of this book to become better acquainted with their use.

The size of your workshop should be determined by your available space and your demands. If you plan to restore one piece at a time, you might only need a six-foot workbench in the corner of your garage or basement. If, however, you succumb to the temptation to buy Arts & Crafts bargains at a faster pace than you can restore them, your car may soon be permanently parked in the driveway.

When selecting a location for your workshop, make sure you can safely vent outdoors the fumes and dust you create. You can make a simple, sturdy workbench from construction grade 2x4's, carriage bolts, and a sheet of three-quarter inch plywood, designing it to fit the space you have selected, then anchoring it to the wall and floor. The width and height of your workbench are critical. Make sure your bench is wide enough (30" min.) to accommodate chairs, rockers, and small tables. The height should be determined by your own, for a workbench which is too low causes chronic backache. Standing next to your kitchen counter should help you decide what the most comfortable working height is for you.

EQUIPMENT

____ workbench	____ storage cabinet
____ metal trash can	____ overhead lighting
____ electrical outlets	____ fans
____ pegboard	____ radio

TOOLS

____ screwdrivers	____ pliers
____ claw hammer	____ electric drill
____ tape measure	____ clamps
____ hobby knife	____ single-edge razor blades
____ scissors	____ chisel
____ metal file	____ nail punch
____ cotton swabs	____ stirring sticks
____ cheesecloth	____ cotton rags
____ dropcloths	____ brushes

ABRASIVES

____ medium (#100) sandpaper
____ medium-fine (#150-#180) sandpaper
____ fine (#220) sandpaper
____ super-fine (#400-#600) sandpaper

____ coarse (#2 or #3) steel wool
____ medium (#0) steel wool
____ fine (#000 or #0000) steel wool

____ medium synthetic sanding pad
____ fine synthetic finishing pad

STAINING

____ aniline dyes (assortment of colors)
____ oil-based stains (reds and browns)
____ 26% ammonia (fuming only)
____ tannic acid crystals (fuming old wood)
____ paste filler
____ universal tints

FINISHING

____ liquid (amber) or flake shellac
____ denatured alcohol (shellac solvent and thinner)
____ interior varnish (non-polyurethane)
____ mineral spirits (low-quality varnish thinner)
____ turpentine (high-quality varnish thinner)
____ boiled linseed oil (varnish additive)
____ paste wax (preferably dark)
____ liquid wax (preferably dark)

OTHER

____ paint and varnish remover
____ 3-ring notebook and pen (documenting formulas)
____ empty glass jars with lids (mixing)
____ box of self-sealing sandwich bags (for hardware)
____ masking tape
____ oak boards (scraps for testing)

SAFETY

____ protective glasses   ____ apron
____ particle mask   ____ respirator
____ lightweight rubber gloves   ____ heavy rubber gloves
____ first-aid kit   ____ fire extinguisher

WORKING CONDITIONS

All furniture finishes are affected by the conditions in which they are applied. If the temperature drops below 60 degrees, your solvents, such as denatured alcohol and mineral spirits, evaporate so slowly the finish may never properly harden. If the humidity rises above 75%, the same thing may happen. In the ideal working environment, the relative humidity should remain between 40% - 60% and the air temperature between 65 - 80 degrees.

All finishes have a *tack time*, which is from the moment the finish leaves the brush or rag to when dust will no longer stick to it. The tack time is affected by the ingredients in the finish as well as by the temperature and humidity in your workshop. Since every finish has a tack time, it is imperative to control the dust in your work area.

Dust can be traced to any of six sources: the air, the wood, the finish, the applicator, your clothes, and your ventilation system.

AIR — A frantic once-a-month cleaning just before you apply a finish is apt to stir up more dust than it will remove. Get into the habit of keeping your work area clean. Sweep and dust on a regular basis. Don't overlook hanging light fixtures, for they can drop dust into a wet finish.

WOOD — The pores of oak are large enough to hide particles of dust until your finish drives them out. A dry rag won't remove them, so use a tack rag to pick them up. You can buy prepared tack rags or you can make your own by adding a few tablespoons of a 50/50 mixture of varnish and mineral spirits to a small section of cheesecloth. Work the mixture into the cloth until it becomes sticky, then store in a small, tightly-sealed container. Wear rubber gloves while making and using a tack cloth or your hands will become as tacky as your cloth.

FINISH — The only can of finish which is guaranteed to be dust-free is an unopened can of finish. A dusty stirring stick or dirty brush will contaminate a fresh can of finish. Dust in the air will land in an open can. After stirring, pour a small amount of finish into a clean container, such as a plastic bowl or coffee cup. Immediately place the lid back on the can. Never pour any leftover finish back into the can, for it will contain dust carried back from the wood by your brush. If you mix your own finish or have any doubts about it, use several layers of cheesecloth or a commercial paint strainer to filter out any dust.

APPLICATOR— Regardless how thorough you may be, a used brush is apt to have particles of dust and dried finish clinging to the bristles, waiting to slide into your wet finish. Start each finish project with a new brush, but don't assume it's clean. Dip the bristles into the solvent for the finish you are using, then brush out the solvent and the dust onto a piece of cardboard. Store your new brushes and finish rags in plastic bags; recycle used finish brushes by cleaning and using them for staining or stripping.

CLOTHES — If you are wearing the same clothes to finish your Stickley table as you wore earlier to sand it, you are a likely source of dust. As you move around the project, dust on your sleeves is going to drop into the finish. Before you start, change into a clean shirt, apron, or jeans. Better yet, slip on a long-sleeved lab coat you keep stored in a closed drawer or cabinet.

VENTILATION — You can't apply a finish without disposing of the fumes, but a stream of fresh air is apt to bring with it particles of dust. Set up a fan to force the air and fumes out of an exterior door or window. Make sure the source of fresh air on the opposite side is not bringing with it additional dust. You may want to tape a furnace filter over a window opening to capture unwanted dust. Run your ventilation fans for several minutes to give them time to eliminate fine particles of dust in the air, on the floor, and on the blades.

Here are a few more tips:

- Elevate your project, placing it on your workbench, across sawhorses, or on concrete blocks. Dust and toxic fumes settle to the floor, so why work there?

- Block any cold air return vents in your workshop to prevent fumes from reaching your furnace.

- Use inexpensive, clip-on reflector lights to direct light exactly where you need it. It is easier to move a light than it is a sticky Morris chair.

- Always work facing your brightest source of light. Light reflecting across a fresh finish will instantly reveal any dry spots, runs, or drips.

- Get a vacuum with a bristle attachment for your workshop. It works better than a broom, dust cloth, or tack rag for permanently removing dust.

- Use clear, self-sealing food storage bags for parts, slivers, hardware, and screws. Place a piece of paper clearly identifying the object in the bag with it.

- Start each project with a fresh can of finish, a fresh rag, and a fresh brush. Why risk a thousand dollar Limbert table trying to save a few bucks on a brush?

- Scour yard sales and auctions not just for Arts & Crafts furniture, but for old tools. You can never have enough clamps or tools, and many older models are far superior to the new ones.

- Get a shallow, stiff plastic tub intended for mixing concrete to use as a stripping pan. Its lightweight, easy to store, and unaffected by paint and varnish remover.

WORKSHOP SAFETY

You have to assume that all wood finishing and refinishing products are potential hazards to your health and safety. Many stains, polishes, and varnishes contain boiled linseed oil, which can self-ignite through spontaneous combustion. While safe in a can or on the wood, if boiled linseed oil or any food finishing oil is left on a rag which is wadded up and tossed in a trash can, the heat generated within the rag by the chemical action taking place as the finish dries can reach the ignition point. The rag bursts into flames, which immediately feed on the oil-soaked fibers.

In addition, the fumes produced by the solvents you will be using can damage your lungs and your brain cells. They are also flammable and can ignite from a tiny spark within a light switch or from a pilot light in a furnace or hot water heater.

Protect your eyes, your lungs, your skin, your home, and your family from toxic fumes and liquids. Run your ventilation fans. Wear protective glasses and a respirator. Store all wood finishing products inside locked cabinets or on high shelves away from your children, pets, furnace, and water heater. Place *all* used rags in a sealed, water-filled container, then put it and all refinishing refuse in a metal, outdoor trash receptacle located away from any building.

What is the cost of carelessness?

Blindness, respiratory failure, skin cancer, and fire.

IDENTIFYING AN ORIGINAL FINISH
25.

When asked to speak on furniture finishing and refinishing, I like to hand my audience a set of twelve boards, each coated with a different finish, yet only identified by a number. I encourage them to touch, feel, smell, even taste each board, then ask them to identify the twelve different finishes. My audiences have included furniture refinishers, professional cabinetmakers, and finish manufacturers, but rarely has anyone correctly identified more than four of the twelve finishes.

My point is simple: most wood finishes look nearly identical.

Despite their similar appearances, however, each finish has its own strengths and weaknesses, making it suitable for one application, but unsuitable for another. Each can also be distinguished by its age and relationship to specific furniture styles and time periods. Modern nitrocellulose lacquer and polyurethane varnish, for instance, did not exist during the Arts & Crafts era, hence are historically inappropriate for Stickley, Limbert, and Roycroft furniture. The Great Wall of China was finished with tung oil, but it was rarely used by Arts & Crafts furniture manufacturers. Of the twelve finishes now available, Arts & Crafts furniture manufacturers and craftsmen displayed a preference for three: shellac, varnish, and wax.

But in the years which have elapsed since Arts & Crafts first fell out of favor, many original shellac, varnish, and wax finishes have been replaced by modern lacquer, oil varnish, spar varnish, polyurethane varnish, Danish oil, or tung oil — many of which look nearly alike.

So how can we distinguish between an original Arts & Crafts finish and a more recent replacement?

You begin with a basic premise: Just as there is no perfect crime, there is no perfect refinisher. Every refinisher will leave behind some clue to his work. If you know what to look for and where to look, you will be able to determine if someone has removed or altered an original finish.

Among the refinishing clues to look for are:

- cross-grain sanding scratches at the intersection of two boards
- old, dark finish in corners and joints
- sandpaper or steel wool scratches in the hardware
- damaged screw heads
- drips, runs, and stripper 'scars' under rungs and arms and down backs and drawer bottoms
- droplets of dried finish beneath an arm or stretcher
- a different finish under a pull than next to it
- a different finish inside a bookcase, desk, or case piece than on the outside
- veneer patches, filled holes, or other repairs
- a dark box of old finish around the shopmark.

Always perform your inspection in bright, natural light or using a flashlight and magnifying glass. Turn the piece upside down, for the most incriminating clues will be located on the underside of stretchers, aprons, and arms. While one clue is not solid proof a piece has been refinished, it should inspire you to a closer inspection, which may lead to the discovery of additional clues.

THE SWAB TEST

You can identify some finishes by determining which solvent will dissolve them. The swab test, however, should not be performed unless absolutely necessary, for done improperly it can damage an original finish. When the test is required, perform it only in an inconspicuous spot, such as behind a stretcher or inside a drawer. Proceed carefully and cautiously, testing only a small spot. Afterwards, don't wipe the test spot, for you could remove the finish. Instead, allow it to dry.

The swab test requires a half-dozen cotton swabs and the solvents listed below. Starting with the mildest (mineral spirits), dip the cotton swab into the solvent, then gently rub the moistened tip on the finish. If the finish begins to dissolve, it will discolor the tip. By referring to the chart below, you should be able to identify the finish by the solvent which softens it.

SOLVENT		FINISH
Mineral Spirits	only dissolves	Wax
Denatured Alcohol	only dissolves	Shellac
Lacquer Thinner	only dissolves	Lacquer and Shellac
Methylene Chloride*	dissolves	All of the Above Modern Lacquer Polyurethane

* the active ingredient in many
paint and varnish removers

Penetrating oil finishes, such as linseed oil and tung oil, are unaffected by any of these solvents, for their resins remain locked in the pores of the wood. Oil finishes, however, can be identified by their dull luster, unique odor, and the lack of any surface buildup. Arts & Crafts furniture manufacturers seldom used oil finishes, for penetrating oils do not fill the open pores of oak as well as do the surface finishes.

ALTERED FINISHES

Original finishes don't always survive in their original condition. Setting aside for the moment finishes which have been naturally altered through normal wear, we need to realize that many original finishes have been lightened, cleaned, topcoated, or enhanced — all in the name of 'restoration.'

Even a thin original finish is still an original finish. Once it has been topcoated with a new finish, such as a fresh coat of shellac, lacquer, or varnish, it becomes an "enhanced" or "restored" original finish. The exception is paste wax, for wax is a reversible material which can be removed with mineral spirits without endangering the original finish beneath it. Protecting an original finish with paste wax is preferred over any other finish, including shellac , for once the new shellac bonds with the original shellac, they cannot be separated. The original shellac finish is, in effect, consumed by the new shellac. Paste wax is more like a polish than a finish and does not diminish the value of an original finish.

You need to be able to recognize and, if possible, correct an altered finish; if that is not possible, the only proper alternative is to duplicate the original finish.

More detailed steps for the restoration of altered finishes are provided in later chapters.

SHELLAC TOPCOAT — During an earlier era marked by ritualist spring cleanings, people often brushed additional coats of fast-drying shellac onto their worn furniture. After several coats, the finish became thick and glossy. Although denatured alcohol will remove the new shellac, it won't distinguish between new shellac and original shellac. A safer method involves removing the new shellac with fine sandpaper or steel wool.

VARNISH TOPCOAT — When varnish began to replace shellac, people began brushing varnish or a combination varnish-stain onto their furniture. Like shellac, it appears glossy, cloudy, and occasionally colored. The only practical solvent for oil-based varnish is methylene chloride, which will dissolve old shellac instantaneously. It is nearly impossible to remove paint or polyurethane varnish with methylene chloride without also removing some of the original finish. A slower, but more controllable method is friction, using either steel wool or fine sandpaper. It isn't fast or easy, but if the piece is worth the effort, do it.

HEAVILY CLEANED — Tabletops and the arms of chairs seem to suffer the most from strong cleansers, gradually sacrificing most of their finish and color to household detergents and water. The loss of color, if not dramatic, may be acceptable, for we should expect a ninety-year old antique to display some signs of wear. If necessary, as you will learn later, lost color can be replaced.

LIGHTENED — The introduction of non-methylene chloride antique refinishers, which are blends of volatile solvents, including denatured alcohol, mineral spirits, acetate, and lacquer thinner, enabled owners to lighten an original finish without resorting to a heavy-bodied paint and varnish remover. As a result, many original finishes were partially removed, leaving behind a thin, fragile layer of finish. Today these finishes are often described as "cleaned, scrubbed, or lightened" original finishes. If they have not been topcoated with a new finish, the description is accurate. The solution is the same as outlined in the previous paragraph: paste wax.

CATHERS & DEMBROSKY

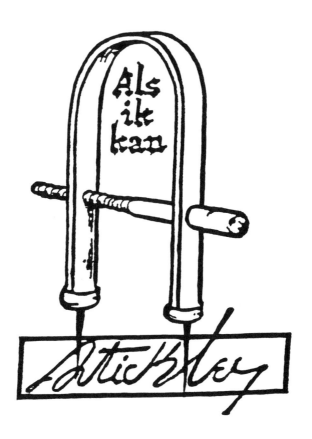

It is in the details.

PO Box 502   Tenafly, New Jersey   07670
(201) 894–8140   (FAX) 569–0946

FINDING AND PROTECTING SHOPMARKS 31.

It should be borne in mind that each piece
of Craftsman furniture is not only tagged
with the name 'Craftsman,' but is stamped
with my registered shopmark — a joiner's
compass of ancient make, enclosing the motto
"Als ik kan," and bearing my signature below.

— Gustav Stickley

Arts & Crafts manufacturers and craftsmen were not the first to affix a shopmark to their work, but never before had the practice been so widespread. Nearly every furniture craftsman from the West Coast to the East designed their own unique marks, which today enable collectors to identify with relative certainty the source of their antiques.

Like an original finish, though, time has not been kind to many shopmarks. Paper labels have proven to be the most fragile, followed closely by transparent decals. Dip-stripping practices, popular during the 1960s and 1970s, destroyed many shopmarks, but the return of more sensitive hand-stripping in recent years has increased the survival rate. Using any of a number of Arts & Crafts reference books, collectors can identify even a fragment of a decal or a scrap of paper label still clinging to a rusty tack.

Collectors have learned, though, that they cannot rely solely on shopmarks for identification, for numerous counterfeit examples have surfaced. Shopmarks should confirm what a comparison to an illustration or to known construction techniques would suggest. Finding a Gustav Stickley paper label on a Larkin desk doesn't make it a Stickley desk any more than pasting Abraham Lincoln's face on a one dollar bill would make it worth five.

Our first priority is to locate the shopmark on any piece we are about to restore. Some manufacturers were very consistent regarding location. Given an arm, the workers at the Limbert factory were apt to put a brand under it; given a drawer, Gustav Stickley's craftsmen preferred to place their brand or decal on it. With the notable exception of the Roycrofters, most furniture shops followed Gustav Stickley's example, placing their shopmarks "in an unobtrusive place." Just as one might expect from the flamboyant Elbert Hubbard, the shopmark for Roycroft furniture will often be carved deep into the splashboard, crestrail, or apron.

When searching for shopmarks, bear in mind furniture manufacturers did not want to hide them from their customers. The location had to be visible, yet not distracting. Many times the type of shopmark determined the location. A metal tag was more apt to be nailed on the unfinished side of an apron than on a stretcher. You are more apt to find large paper labels glued or tacked to the backs of bookcases than inside a door. Small decals gave the craftsmen more flexibility in selecting a location, for a postage stamp decal could be placed on the outside of a leg or stretcher, underneath an arm, or on the inside of a china cabinet.

With these thoughts in mind (and the knowledge that not every piece was marked!), arm yourself with a flashlight and magnifying glass, for many shopmarks will have faded or have been partially destroyed with cleaning agents or solvents. If the piece has been painted, use a single-edged razor blade to careful scrape off the paint over an area where you would expect to find a shopmark.

SEARCHING FOR SHOPMARKS

Chairs, Footstools, and Settles
- under an arm
- inside or outside a rear stretcher, often next to a leg
- underneath the seat
- on the lower portion of a leg
- inside an apron or seat frame

Tabourets and Tables
- under the top
- on a stretcher

Sideboards, Servers, Library Tables, Dressers, and Desks
- inside or outside a drawer side
- top or bottom of a drawer bottom
- exterior, upper center of the back

China Cabinets and Bookcases
- exterior, upper center of the back
- interior, upper center of the back
- inside a door, at the top
- interior, top of either side

Beds
- inside a rail
- inside lower board on footboard
- exterior, back of headboard

Note: Exceptions abound, so do not limit yourself to these locations. Start here, but do not stop searching until you are convinced the piece was not or is no longer marked.

PROTECTING A SHOPMARK

The degree of protection required by a shopmark during restoration will depend on the type of shopmark and the chemicals being used on the piece. Fortunately, the condition of the shopmark, provided it can be identified, has no bearing on the value of the antique. A fragment is just as important as an entire label. Nevertheless, you should never subject any shopmark to potential damage from paint and varnish remover or any solvent. A careless swipe with a rag loaded with denatured alcohol can make a decal disappear before your eyes.

Regardless of the type of shopmark and the extent of your restoration work, observe these three basic rules:

#1. Never trust masking tape.
Tape only provides you with a false sense of security, for most solvents will quickly seep under or through masking tape. Many refinishers become careless, assuming the tape is protecting the mark. Later they discover the solvent had seeped under the tape and ruined the shopmark.

#2. Never apply an adhesive material to a shopmark.
The adhesive in any tape can pull the lettering off a paper label or decal.

#3. Never apply a finish to a paper label.
A coat of finish makes old paper even more brittle, shortening its life expectancy.

To protect a shopmark during the restoration process, begin by testing your painter's masking tape (a special type with less adhesive on it; available at paint stores) on an inconspicuous spot to make sure it does not remove any finish. Then cut an oversized piece of stiff, clear acetate (available in craft stores) to cover and extend one inch beyond the shopmark. Secure the acetate over the shopmark with the masking tape.

The acetate will protect the shopmark from splatters, spills, dropped tools, and dirty fingers. Since it is clear, a quick glance will reveal if any solvent has seeped underneath the masking tape. When all of the work is done except for that area under the acetate, carefully remove the tape and the acetate and give the area your total concentration. When removing an old finish, use cotton swabs or inexpensive artist brushes to carefully apply the solvent; single-edged razor blades and more cotton swabs are ideal for removing the old finish around the shopmark. A bright light and magnifying glass assure professional results. Here are a few more specific tips:

Metal tags: Don't attempt to remove them. Your pliers or screwdriver will damage the heads of the tacks, leaving the impression that someone transferred the tag from another piece of furniture. • Don't rub the metal with a solvent rag, for the solvent may remove the natural patina. • Don't brush a finish over the metal shopmark, for the finish will eventually discolor and peal.

Paper Labels: Don't attempt to remove them, for they tear easily. • Glue down any loose or torn areas using a thin solution of household glue and a sliver of wood as an applicator. • Never use scotch tape to repair a paper label, for the tape will eventually turn yellow, peel, and scar the paper. • Protect brittle labels permanently with an oversized piece of acetate held in place with four upholstery tacks; keeping the edges of the acetate unsealed allows the paper to breathe and avoids condensation of moisture around the paper.

Brands: Don't assume you can sand over them, for some are very shallow. • What appears to be a permanent brand might be a fragile black decal or rubber-stamp ink.

Decals: Never wipe over a decal with a solvent rag. • Never apply a finish over a decal, for the solvent may dissolve the decal. • Never rub a decal with a rag and rubbing compound or fine steel wool. It may disappear. • Dab, don't rub, the decal with paste wax to protect it.

The art dealers formerly known as Duke

CAROL GRANT / ANN DUKE
DECORATIVE ARTS

Grant
(248)543-3580

Duke
(248)547-5511

MAKING REPAIRS
37.

Never replace that which you can repair;
never repair that which you can refinish;
never refinish that which you can restore;
never restore that which you can clean;
never clean that which you can use.

— anonymous

The time to make a repair is as soon as you discover it, for as you wait, edges become dulled, slivers lost, and other joints loosen. I prefer to make repairs prior to stripping off an inappropriate finish for the same reasons. In addition, here are some other general guidelines before we get into specifics:

- Only use old wood for duplicating lost parts, filling holes, patching gouges, and patching veneer. Never use wood dough, for it does not accept stains and finishes like wood.
- Take the time to select a donor patch or board which matches the grain of the surrounding wood; you can always change the color of the wood, but you can never change the pattern of the grain.
- You can never have too many clamps; watch for them at yard sales and consignment auctions.
- Use disposable syringes (available from your physician or veterinary) to inject glue into pinned but loose joints and under veneer bubbles.
- Do it once, do it right.

Burns - Carefully scrape off any charred finish and wood fibers using an Xacto knife. Shallow burns may be disguised using an artist brush and paints, meticulously duplicating missing pores, flakes, and color. Deeper burns should be filled with a veneer patch (see *Veneer* repairs). Avoid wood dough or wood putty.

Cracks - Boards generally crack when placed under extreme stress, as when a mover drops a $363,000 sideboard, or when boards dry out and shrink. Stress fractures are easier to repair, for the two sides will generally want to go back together. Shrinkage fractures are more difficult and may be hindered by screws, nails, or tenons on either side of the split. If the two sides can be pushed together, swab both exposed edges with woodworking glue, then clamp them together under moderate pressure for 24 hours. Immediately wipe off any excess glue with a damp rag. And always protect the antique from the jaws of the clamps with scraps of soft wood.

A shrinkage crack, commonly found on legs, backs, table leaves, and plank sides, may defy all glues, springing back as soon as the clamps are released. If the crack is serious and demands attention, remove any nearby screws or nails to free the board. After clamping, you may need to drill new screw holes. If you cannot remove or clamp a cracked board, you may need to cut, sand, and glue in a tapered strip of wood. Minor cracks of a superficial nature may be disguised with dark paste wax, but never use any synthetic wood filler or wood dough. The inevitable movement between the two sides will crack the filler and grind it into powder.

Dents - A dent is compressed wood pores. If the dent is shallow, you may be able to enlarge the crushed fibers by placing a drop of water in the depression. Since standing water can damage a finish — especially an old finish — you should only attempt this on a piece which is also being refinished. Otherwise, dents are like a member of the family; you simply have to live with them.

Gouges - A gouge is missing wood. You don't have to live with it. But a gouge cannot properly be repaired with wood dough.

Use an Xacto knife to clean out the gouge, removing loose fibers and squaring up the sides in preparation for the wood patch. An irregular patch is less obvious than a square or rectangle, but takes longer to fit. Since you aren't being paid by the hour, take the time to do it right. Select your patch carefully from wood (1) the same age, (2) the same basic color, and (3) with the same grain pattern. Trim and shape the gouge and the patch using your knife, a fine file, and sandpaper until the two fit together as snugly as pieces in a puzzle. To insure a good color match, color your patch before you clamp it in place.

Loose Joints - Pegged joints never fall apart, but they can wobble. Regluing any other style of furniture is far easier, for you simply pull or tap the joint apart, scrape off the old glue, apply fresh glue, then clamp it. With Arts & Crafts furniture, dismantling a joint by removing a peg is a last resort, for it can rarely be done without destroying the peg and damaging the hole. Do not let any refinisher drill out the pegs to reglue a joint, for an antique with replaced pegs might as well have an albatross hung around its neck.

To reglue a pegged joint, use a syringe to inject glue into the joint. If you move the loose board in every direction possible, you can slide the needle past the tenon and into the mortise. If necessary, drill a hole no larger than the needle diameter into the mortise, positioning the hole on inside of the joint where it will be less noticeable. Inject glue into the mortise and apply pressure on the joint with clamps for 24 hours. Afterwards, disguise the hole with a dab of dark paste wax .

Removing Pegs - A peg may have to be removed to replace a badly damaged board or shortened leg. It is impossible to drill out a peg using the same diameter bit without damaging the hole. Instead, drill a 1/8-inch pilot hole approximately one inch deep in the center of the peg. Insert a wood screw into the pilot hole, then, using a claw hammer or pry bar atop a piece of scrap wood, slowly apply pressure to the screw just as if you were removing a nail from a board. As the screw rises out of the board, it will bring the peg along with it, for the threads of the screw imbedded in the oak are generally stronger than the old glue. As the screw and peg rise, place additional scraps of wood under your hammer or pry bar to prevent it from pulling at an angle and damaging the lip of the hole.

Replacing Pegs - When making a major repair or replacing inappropriate pegs, you have to start by realizing not all pegs begin as dowels. Manufactured dowels available at hardware stores have two drawbacks. First, they are always slightly smaller than the listed diameter, hence a 3/8-inch dowel does not fit snugly in a 3/8-inch hole. Second, the visible portion of a peg made from a dowel is end grain, but if you look closely at your Arts & Crafts antique, you may find the pegs were cut from side grain. The difference won't seem important until you apply a stain, dye, or finish to an end-grain dowel. When it turns nearly black, everyone will know it's new.

To make a side-grain peg you will need a plug-cutting attachment for an electric drill. Since the plugs will only be approximately one-half inch long, you will also need to use a manufactured dowel cut one-half inch shorter than the depth of the hole. Tap the manufactured dowel into the glue-swabbed hole until it is one-half inch below the surface, then insert your side-grain plug cut from an old oak board into the remaining space. The manufactured dowel provides the necessary strength, the plug provides the necessary look. You can sand the face of the plug before you slide it into the hole, or allow it to protrude and sand it flush with the wood after the glue dries.

Tip: If a new peg does not fit snugly inside the hole, place a drop or two of water on it. As the cells absorb the water they will swell, pressing against the fresh glue on the side of the hole. As it dries, the glue will lock the plug in its expanded condition.

Rings and Spots - Black rings are in the wood; white rings are in the finish. Removing a black ring from the wood beneath an existing finish is impossible without risking damage to the finish. Black rings must be attacked with bleach, thus most collectors postpone this procedure until the piece is being completely refinished. Once the wood is bare and sanded, apply either wood bleach, household bleach, or a saturated solution of oxalic acid crystals in warm water to the black ring or spot. Allow 24 hours for the bleach to work, then rinse with vinegar to neutralize the bleach and then with water to flush off the vinegar. After the wood dries, sand to smooth the raised grain.

White rings can be removed from a finish, but unless done carefully and cautiously, you can damage the finish. A fresh white ring should be left alone, for the trapped moisture may evaporate. To speed the evaporation, use a hair drier to direct warm air across the ring. Do not rub the white ring with oil, polish, or wax, any of which will seal the moisture in the finish. Old white rings which refuse to evaporate may be rubbed out using #600-grit sandpaper saturated in a light-weight dusting oil, such as mineral oil, lemon oil, or cedar oil. Do not use tung oil or any other furniture finish. Keeping the surface and the sandpaper saturated with the lubricating oil, gently wet-sand the entire top rather than just the white ring. Afterwards, wipe the piece dry. The following day restore the lost sheen with paste wax (see page 83).

If the white ring persists, then it can only be eliminated by removing or dissolving the finish. Obviously, leaving the white ring (which may still grow fainter or disappear over time) is preferable over removing an original finish.

Rot - All rot, including dry rot, is caused by moisture. Soft, rotted wood should only be removed as a last resort. Begin by stabilizing the wood with an application of a commercial wood hardener. Follow the manufacture's directions and precautions closely. Afterwards replace any missing wood with actual wood (see *gouges*); wood fillers soon crumble under the weight of the furniture.

To redistribute the weight placed on a rotted foot, turn the piece on its back and drill a 3/8-inch or 1/2-inch hole into the bottom of the soft foot. Drill through the entire length of soft wood, stopping only when your bit reaches solid wood. Swab the inside of the hole with glue, then tap in a dowel longer than the depth of the hole. Saw the dowel off 1/8-inch above the bottom of the rotted foot so that the weight of the furniture rests on the dowel rather than the soft foot. If necessary, compensate for the increased height by nailing furniture glides on the bottoms of the other feet (which is also a safe and easy way to compensate for a sloping floor).

Scratches - Nicks and scratches can be disguised with colored wax, an oil-based stain applied with a fine artist's brush, or with felt-tipped pens. The pens contain permanent dyes in an assortment of colors and the fine tips are even more accurate than artist's brushes. If a repaired scratch or nick dries to a dull color, replace the lost sheen using paste wax. Make sure the color you applied is dry, or the rubbing action of your rag will remove it.

Veneer - Despite the widely-held belief that mission oak furniture, particularly that of the Stickleys', is all "solid" oak, nearly every Arts & Crafts manufacturer utilized veneer to some degree on wide doors, sides, and, less frequently, on tops. Experience has demonstrated that wide boards tend to warp. Several narrow boards glued together won't warp, but they don't look as attractive as a single board. The compromise was discovered centuries ago: construct the door of several narrow boards selected for their strength rather than beauty, then cover each side with wide sheets of highly-figured veneer.

When replacing or repairing veneer, it is critical to match the original in grain pattern, color, thickness, and age. You can purchase new veneer or you can use wet towels to soak old veneer off discarded drawer fronts and sides of ruined Victorian dressers. Though it borders on cannibalism, professional restorers have been known to cut a small donor patch from a hidden spot on the antique they are repairing, such as from under a desk or from the top of an inside leg. They make their primary repair using the veneer taken from the antique and use new veneer to patch the spot where they harvested their donor. They are willing to make two repairs in order to make the primary repair nearly invisible.

Veneer Bubbles - Carefully slice the bubble with an Xacto knife, then carefully squirt or slide glue under the bubble. Press down on the bubble to distribute the glue under the entire area and force out the air. Wipe off any excess glue, cover with wax paper, and clamp or stack with weights to force the veneer against the wood for 24 hours. The wax paper will prevent any escaping glue from attaching your weights to the antique.

Veneer Chips - Take the time to cut and glue veneer patches, for synthetic fillers never match authentic wood. Square the sides of the damaged area with a fresh blade for a snug fit. Joint lines around the patch are less noticeable if they run in the same direction as the grain. Avoid rectangular or square patches; if necessary, enlarge the damaged area slightly to accept a diamond-shaped or triangular patch. Use masking tape to clamp small veneer patches along the edge of a door or drawer.

Veneer, Loose - Clean out any loose particles of old, dried glue with a long dinner knife or putty knife. Gently lift the veneer a fraction of an inch while you inject or spread glue under the loose veneer. Press into place to distribute the glue evenly, taking care to force glue into the deepest recesses. Wipe off the excess glue, then clamp or weight for 24 hours.

Veneer, Missing - I have seen legs, aprons, and even tops with veneer damage so extreme the only possible solution seemed to be to remove all of the veneer by soaking it under wet towels for three days. If you are absolutely positive it cannot be repaired, remove the remaining old veneer, saving it for future repairs. Do not fall prey to the temptation to refinish the wood beneath the veneer, for pores which have been saturated with glue never respond well to a dye, stain, or finish. Take the time to cut, color, glue, and finish new veneer to replace the old.

 # VOORHEES CRAFTSMAN

FURNITURE   ART POTTERY   ACCESSORIES

Exhibiting Daily:

Northern California: Antique Society 2661 Gravenstein
Highway South   Sebastopol, CA 95472
Southern California: Santa Monica Antique Market
1607 Lincoln Blvd. Santa Monica, CA 90404

For Warehouse Appointment, Photos or Information,
call Steve and Mary Ann Voorhess at (707) 584-5044 or
fax (707) 584-3502.

WOOD PREPARATION
45.

A finish can only be as smooth
as the wood that's under it.

- anonymous

You can skip this chapter, IF

- you never plan to strip any furniture
- you never plan to make any furniture
- you never plan to buy any unfinished furniture
- you never plan to make any replacement parts.

If, however, you are diving deep beneath the surface of an Arts & Crafts finish, then you may want to take with you some basic information on preparing the wood for a stain, dye or finish.

Critical to duplicating an Arts & Crafts finish is knowing how to prepare the wood for your finish. Without the proper preparation, your finish is apt to (1) never dry, (2) never stick, or (3) never look right. Fortunately, wood is very forgiving. It will surrender a coat of white paint, respond to a brisk sanding, and absorb yet another application of stain. It gives us not only a second chance, but a third and fourth, if needed. No other material as plentiful, including clay, plastic, copper, and glass, is as easy to work with or as forgiving when damaged.

STRIPPING
46.

Nearly a century of use and abuse has proven that Arts & Crafts furniture does not wear out. Those who dislike the style cannot fault the construction. Pinned joints, splined tops, and keyed tenons insured its longevity, but when the Arts & Crafts style slipped from fashion's plate, reluctant owners took many liberties with the finish. Painting and pickling were two of the favorite, with the color choice reflecting the prevailing style. After 1970, when Golden Oak made a strong comeback, many examples of Arts & Crafts furniture were dipped, bleached, sanded, and encased in a thick amber coat of varnish.

When faced with either a painted or polyurethaned piece, the only practical alternative is to use a strong paint and varnish remover to soften the inappropriate finish. Today there are three major types of finish removers on the market:

- traditional methylene chloride paint and varnish removers (Zip-Strip, Parks, or Red Devil)
- new non-methylene chloride paint and varnish removers (3-M's Safe Stripper)
- blends of thin, fast-evaporating solvents, including denatured alcohol, toluene, naptha, and lacquer thinner (Minwax Antique Furniture Refinisher)

Of the three types, only the methylene chloride removers can soften paint and polyurethane efficiently. The active ingredients in the "safe" strippers, while less threatening to the user, may need several hours, if not days, to completely soften a thick coat of paint or polyurethane varnish. The solvent strippers simply evaporate before they have a chance to soften paint or tough polyurethane varnish.

Selecting the best brand of paint and varnish remover is compounded by the realization that some brands work better on certain types of paint than others. The best advice is to experiment with different brands until you find the one that works the best for you. Stick with it until you run into a finish that it won't budge, then try another.

As obvious as it sounds, the single most common mistake people make is not following the directions on the can, including the safety precautions. Pumped with excitement, many people don't give the freshly applied paint and varnish remover adequate time to attack the hardened resins. After only a few minutes they begin to poke at it, peek under it, and probe the old finish to see what is underneath. Each time they do, they break the barrier protecting the methylene chloride from the air. Oxygen causes the methylene chloride to evaporate before it has a chance to soften the paint. As a result, the paint stays on the wood — and the consumer swears the brand of remover is weak and ineffective.

STEPS FOR STRIPPING

1. Protect the shopmark with an oversized sheet of acetate.
2. Remove all hardware using the proper size screwdriver.
3. Remove any drawers, doors, cushions, leaves, or lids.
4. Position the antique so that the section you are stripping is horizontal; the remover will work better in a puddle than running down the side.
5. Brush on a thick, generous coat of paint and varnish remover.

6. Allow the stripper to remain undisturbed until it has nearly dried.

7. Carefully scrape off the first layer of softened paint using a putty knife with rounded corners.

8. Analyze the wood: if paint remains in the pores or on the wood, immediately apply a second coat of remover and repeat steps #5-#7; if the wood is nearly clean, proceed to the next step.

> TIP: Use a brass bristle brush (the type used to clean barbecue grills) to remove softened paint from the pores.

9. Dip either a pad of #2 (coarse) steel wool or a synthetic stripping pad into your rinse and begin scrubbing off the remaining paint while it is still soft.

> TIP: Avoid using water as a rinse, for it softens the wood, loosens veneer, and takes days to dry; instead, use denatured alcohol, lacquer thinner, or mineral spirits.

10. Wash each section with a rag dipped in clean rinse (but not water) to remove any traces of wax, remover, and old finish left in the pores.

> TIP: Ask your dentist for a worn-out dental pick to dig soft paint out from joints and around exposed tenons.

11. Wipe completely dry.

In addition to the specific instructions recommended by manufacturers of paint and varnish removers, allow me to offer the following suggestions:

- Follow all safety precautions recommended in this book and by the manufacturer.
- Wear safety glasses and durable rubber gloves from the moment you take the lid off the remover to when you spread your last rag out to dry.
- Keep an extra pair of gloves nearby in case your first pair tears, melts, or snags on a splinter.
- Wear old shoes, for the remover and old paint tend to land on your feet.
- Work where splatters won't cause any damage.
- Avoid direct sunlight, which evaporates stripper.
- Place the piece on blocks of wood so that you can see and reach the bottom of each leg.
- Pad the jaws of pliers with small pieces of self-adhesive felt or masking tape to avoid scratching the patina on pyramid-head screws.
- Be a neat stripper: immediately wipe stripper and rinse off the undersides of arms, tabletops, leaves, drawers, stretchers, etc.
- Strip and refinish both sides of table leaves; this prevents warping and may allow you to press the underside into service if the top side is ever damaged.
- It is easier to strip paint *off* than sand it *out*; don't quit stripping until the last of the paint has been removed.

SANDING
50.

The Industrial Revolution left on our doorsteps an amazing array of sandpapers and labor-saving devices, ranging from papers coarse enough to remove paint to those fine enough to raise a shine on a Steinway. Just as tempting are the electric vibrating toys designed to jiggle, whirl, flog, and oscillate at thousands of revolutions per minute, reducing us to mere manikins standing mindlessly in a cloud of sawdust.

The antique restorer, however, takes a different approach to sanding than does a woodworker. When a woodworker looks at the top of a Stickley library table, he sees scratches. We see patina. Asked to refinish it, the woodworker reaches for a belt sander. We reach for steel wool. Asked to repair it, the woodworker recommends a new top. We go someplace else.

Before we can recognize and control both the good and the evil inherent in sandpaper, we have to understand patina.

Patina is proof of age. It is the difference between a new board and an old board, a new finish and an original finish. Patina consists of hundreds of thousands of tiny scratches created by daily dusting, dining, and drinking. It is a mellowness of colors muted by sunlight. It is an oxidation of all surfaces — wood, metal, glass, and varnish. It is the difference between a baby's cheek and that of her grandfather's.

Every surface can have a patina, including metal, glass, glaze, wood, and its finish. In furniture, we need to realize the wood and the finish have separate patinas. Solvents will destroy the patina of a finish, but not of the wood. Sandpaper, however, can destroy both. Like beauty, patina is only skin deep, and in less than ten seconds, a belt sander and a sheet of 80-grit sandpaper can erase more than one hundred years of history. Regardless how hard we might try, how many tricks we might resort to, we cannot duplicate what only time can achieve.

Sanding Old Wood Which Has Been Stripped

1. Start with #220-grit sandpaper. If it clogs quickly with stripper residue, drop back to #180-grit. Or re-strip.
2. Crease and cut your sheet of sandpaper into fourths. Fold each fourth into a piece small enough to control easily with your fingertips. On flat surfaces, attach the sandpaper to a plastic or rubber sanding block or wrap it around a small block of wood. Do not use electric sanders, for they leave more scratches than they remove. They also destroy patina.
3. Sand only in the direction of the grain. Cross-grain scratches slice through the tubular cell structure of the wood. When you apply a stain or dye, these slices into the tubes actually absorb more liquid, making them stand out.
4. Clean your sandpaper often with a wire brush. Discard the sandpaper whenever it clogs with old finish, for those shiny patches on your sandpaper will leave smudges in the wood.
5. Sand only until the wood is smooth. Stop before you cut through the patina of the wood.

Sanding New Wood

1. Start with #100- or #120-grit to remove machine marks.
2. Step up to #180 and then to #220 to remove the scratches left by your #100 or #120 sandpaper. Orbital and palm sanders are convenient for sanding new wood, but only with #180 or #220 sandpaper. Medium and coarse sandpaper will leave swirling cross-grain scratches in the wood.
3. Follow steps 2-4 above.

> TIP: Use #220-grit sandpaper to duplicate wear in appropriate places on new wood. Study authentic antiques to determine the amount of wear you should imitate.

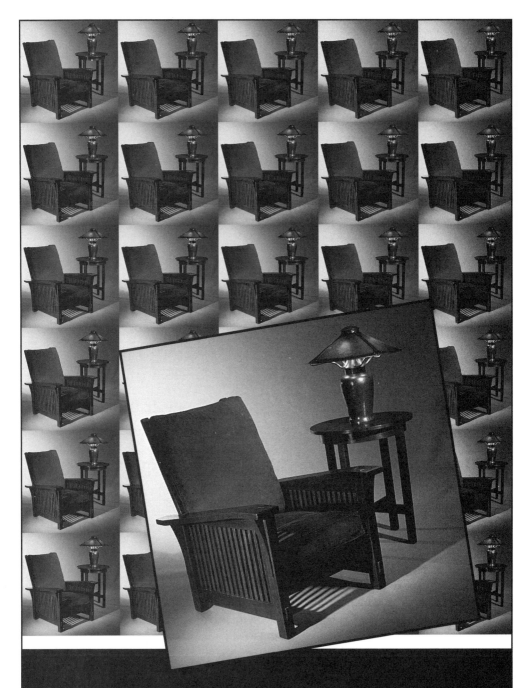

ARTS & CRAFTS COLORS
53.

In the bygone days of the not so very long ago,
the secrets of making these stains were very carefully
guarded and kept as heirlooms, descending from
father to son, or were bought outright and considered as capital in the business. While a few were
good and even today deserve a place at least in the
memory of the finishes, the great majority of these
recipes for stains were very cumbersome, uselessly
loaded down with unnecessary ingredients, and very
inconvenient to make and some of them nearly im-
practicable. Most of them have disappeared and
become obsolete...."

- from *The Modern Wood Finisher* (1900)

N. I. "Sandy" Bienenstock, the legendary historian of 20th-
century furniture manufacturers, observed in his book *A History of American Furniture* that "Mission furniture dictated its
own finish – that of weathered oak. Previous to its introduction, each and every manufacturer took the liberty of finishing
the oak styles of the day in any color he considered fit. Thus,
before the Mission styles there were such colors as Flemish,
which was nearly a dead black, Belgian, Cathedral, Antwerp,
Austrian and other names applied to the gradations of the
Flemish black. All these were manufacturer's designations,
having no authentic relation to the country, city or any other
term applied to it.

"With Mission furniture, it was impossible for the manufacturer to continue using his pet color. The public demanded
the "weathered oak" appearance; and nothing less would

please the purchaser. Manufacturers found it difficult to obtain the formula because there was no record of the formula or the one who concocted it. Efforts to obtain the finish are described in an early trade journal of the period:

"One head finisher is said to have worked for six consecutive weeks, assisted by an expert chemist, endeavoring to find or concoct some combination of acids which would have the same effect on oak that rain and sunshine had. At last his efforts were, in part, repaid, and he announced to his contemporaries that he had been successful. The following day a certain druggist, from whom the successful finisher was supposed to buy his supplies, was puzzled to receive this plaintive note: 'Please deliver to the bearer of this note some of the stain that Mr. Hansen uses to make weathered oak stain.'

"Another manufacturer went to the trouble of buying from a competitor through a retail dealer a small sample of the liquid stain, which he submitted to his chemist for analysis, but was disappointed to discover from the reply that the preparation was too expensive for his grade of work. The chemist did not discover that it contained 85% water and was worth about a dollar a barrel.

"But this was not the process used on fine furniture, where better results were demanded at any cost. This class of work commanded high prices which would admit of much more handling in the finishing room, as well as much longer time for drying."

We can assume, perhaps, that the Stickleys, Limbert, and the Roycrofters would have been categorized as makers of "fine furniture," although we know they each experimented with several different stains, dyes, and finishes. As Bienenstock noted, there were — and still are — several different means of achieving the colors associated with the Arts & Crafts movement. Given the wide range of colors, from dark ebony to a reddish golden oak, the methods vary from fuming to chemical coloring to aniline dyes and oil-based stains, and often included combinations of several standard methods.

FUMING
55.

While several major manufacturers of Arts & Crafts furniture advocated fuming as a first step in their coloring process, no one wrote more about the subject than Gustav Stickley:

"The fact that ammonia fumes will darken new oak was discovered by accident. Some oak boards stored in a stable in England were found after a time to have taken on a beautiful mellow brown tone and on investigation this change in color was discovered to be due to the ammonia fumes that naturally are present in stables.

"The reason for this effect was at first unknown and, to the best of our belief, it was not discovered until the experiments with fuming made in The Craftsman Workshops established the fact that the darkening of the wood was due to the chemical affinity existing between ammonia and tannic acid, of which there is a large percentage present in white oak."

- from *Craftsman Homes* (1909)

Although research has indicated that Gustav Stickley was far from the first to recognize and make use of the "chemical affinity existing between ammonia and tannic acid," he did more than anyone else of his era to describe the process:

"Oak should be ripened as the old mahogany was ripened by oil and sunshine, and this can be done only by a process that, without altering or disguising the nature of the wood, gives it the appearance of having been mellowed by age and use. This process is merely fuming with ammonia, which has a certain affinity with the tannic acid that exists in the wood, and it is the only one known to us that acts upon the glossy hard rays as well as the softer parts of the wood, coloring all together in an even tone so that the figure is marked only by its difference in texture. This result is not so good when stains are used instead of fuming, as staining leaves the soft part of the wood dark and the markings light and prominent.

"Fuming is not an especially difficult process, but requires a good deal of care, for the piece must be put in an airtight box or closet, on the floor of which has been placed shallow dishes containing aqua ammonia (26%). The length of time required to fume oak to a good color depends largely upon the tightness of the compartment, but as a rule 48 hours is enough.

"When fuming is not practical, as in the case of a piece too large for any available compartment or one that is built into the room, a fairly good result may be obtained by applying the strong ammonia directly to the wood with a sponge or brush. In either case the wood must be in its natural condition when treated, as any previous application of oil or stain would keep the ammonia from taking effect. After the wood so treated is thoroughly dry from the first application it should be sandpapered carefully with fine sandpaper, then a second coat of ammonia applied, followed by a second careful sandpapering."

A writer for the Popular Mechanics Company provided additional information in *Mission Furniture: How To Make It*, ca. 1909-1912:

"Darkened oak always has a better appearance when fumed with ammonia. The process is rather a difficult one, as it requires an airtight case. Oak articles can be treated in a case made from a biscuit box, provided it is airtight. The oak to be fumed is arranged in the box so that the fumes will entirely surround the piece. The chief point is to see that no part of the wood is covered up. A saucer of ammonia is placed in the bottom of the box, the lid or cover closed, and all joints sealed up by pasting heavy brown paper over them. Any leakage will be detected if the nose is placed near the tin and further application of the paper will stop the holes. A hole may be cut in the cover and a piece of glass fitted in, taking care to have all the edges closed. The process may be watched through the glass and the article removed when the oak is fumed to the desired shade. Wood stained in this manner should not be French polished or varnished, but waxed."

Neither writer, however, adequately emphasized the dangers associated with 26% ammonia. The fumes alone can cause blindness, lung damage, or death. If the fumes reach a concentration of 25% of the air capacity of the room, they can ignite. Splashing the liquid in your eyes will cause permanent damage to your sight.

For these reasons and more, never experiment with ammonia fuming without:

- a respirator
- rubber gloves
- eye goggles (tight-fitting swimming goggles)
- a long-sleeved shirt
- adequate ventilation

So why subject myself to these dangers when safer stains and dyes are available?

Only because, as Gustav Stickley, Charles Limbert, and Leopold Stickley agreed, no stain or dye can achieve the same results.

Can I achieve *nearly* the same results using standard (2%) household ammonia?

Only if (1) you do not want to achieve a true ebony color, and (2) you are willing to fume the piece for as many as five or six days. I have found that if I placed as many shallow pans of household ammonia as I could fit into my fuming box, to increase the intensity of the fumes around the wood, I could achieve a medium fumed effect after several days. The intensity of the color can be deepened if the wood is first treated with tannic acid (see pg. 59).

What can I use as a fuming box?

Any airtight container, including plastic containers, rubber garbage cans, plastic furniture storage bags, and special tents made from ordinary lumber and 4 ml. plastic. The container must be airtight for your protection and to keep the fumes circulating around the furniture. And the plastic must not touch any portion of the wood, for if it blocks the fumes, that section will emerge lighter than the rest.

Which woods will react to fuming?

Only those with tannin present in the cells. In their natural state, that includes oak and chestnut; to a lesser extent cherry and maple will respond to the fumes of ammonia, turning slightly darker and richer looking. To fume any wood which does not contain tannin, simply follow the directions and precautions on the following page for mixing and applying tannic acid. Always experiment on scrap pieces of wood.

How long should I leave it in?

The amount of time required to achieve a specific shade will be determined by four criteria: (1) the amount of tannin in the lumber, (2) the size of the fuming compartment, (3) the amount of liquid ammonia in the compartment, and (4) the temperature of the air, which determines the evaporation rate of the ammonia and the resulting density of ammonia fumes around the wood. In practice, fuming in a cold basement takes considerably longer than fuming outdoors on a warm, sunny day.

If you going to fume a new piece of furniture or a replacement part you have constructed, first place several test scraps from the same lumber in the fuming box or tent you plan to use. Check the scraps every six hours, removing one each time; brush a finish on each scrap to observe the final color. Label each sample for future reference. Once you have determined the required time to achieve the color you want, repeat the procedure using your actual piece of furniture or replacement part.

If you are fuming an antique, samples of new wood won't be of any help. Instead, check the piece every three hours to inspect the color. Having a clear plastic window in your fuming box or tent will help. Once the color is right, put on your safety equipment, open the tent, and cover the pan of ammonia with a lid. Remove the piece from the fuming tent to stop the chemical action. Immediately open your exterior door and turn on your ventilation fans to clear the room of the escaping fumes. Place the fumed wood outdoors for a few hours while the fumes of the ammonia seep out of the pores.

LOST TANNIN

Arts & Crafts furniture craftsmen enjoyed the advantage of working with new wood. They did not have to worry about patina, original finishes, and the amount of tannin remaining in the cells. We have since discovered that old oak does not contain as much tannin as new oak. It appears the tannin gradually and naturally leaches out of the wood. Without the necessary tannin, antique pieces simply do not respond well to fuming.

This poses a serious problem when faced with an early Arts & Crafts piece which originally had been fumed extremely dark, but which has since been refinished much lighter. No amount of stain or dye can duplicate the effect of intense fuming, yet no amount of ammonia can react with missing tannin.

To compensate, you can easily add tannin to a piece which you have stripped down to bare wood. Begin by ordering tannic acid crystals from a pharmacy or chemical supply company, for you won't find it on the shelves in your local hardware store. To prepare, follow this formula, wearing protective glasses and adjusting the amounts in proportion to the size of your project.

MIXING TANNIC ACID

1. Warm one cup of distilled water.
2. Remove from the heat.
3. One tablespoon at a time, slowly stir in the tannic acid crystals.
4. Continue adding tannic acid crystals until the water reaches a saturated solution (approx. three tablespoons).
5. Pour into a container, then seal and label clearly with the date and ingredients.

REPLACING LOST TANNIN

1. Sand the wood lightly with #220-grit sandpaper until the wood is free from any wax, oil, stripper residue, or old finish.
2. Wipe off the dust with a damp rag.
3. Wearing protective glasses and rubber gloves, brush or sponge a saturated solution of tannic acid onto the entire piece. Work the water-based solution into the pores of the wood. Apply a liberal, yet even coat of tannic acid.
4. Allow 24 hours for the wood to absorb the tannin.
5. On pieces which are to be fumed extremely dark, repeat steps #3 and #4.
6. While wearing a particle mask, sand the dry wood lightly with #220-grit sandpaper to smooth the raised grain.
7. Wipe off the dust with a damp rag.
8. Proceed to the fuming stage.

SAFETY PRECAUTIONS

Tannic acid is not as dangerous as its name implies, provided you follow the proper safety precautions. During use avoid contact with your eyes and skin. Wear protective glasses, appropriate clothing, and rubber gloves. Work only in a well-ventilated area. The dust may prove irritating, so wear long-sleeved clothing and a particle mask when sanding wood treated with tannic acid. Store the container in a locked cabinet when not in use. Wash thoroughly after handling. Follow all safety precautions included on the label or the Material Safety Data Sheet available from the supplier.

ANILINE DYES
61.

If you check the shelves at your local hardware or paint store, you won't find a can or bottle of aniline dye. What was once a staple of every home workshop and furniture factory has now been replaced by pigmented oil-based stains. The reasons are twofold: first, oil-based stains are easier for the novice to control; second, dyes fade faster than pigments.

Yet if you pick up a copy of *Fine Woodworking* or *American Woodworker*, you will find most craftsmen prefer dyes over heavily pigmented wiping stains. Their reasoning is just as understandable: dyes offer more clarity than pigmented stains. The pigments, which are finely ground particles of earth suspended in mineral spirits, lodge in the pores of the wood, where they provide color, but at the sacrifice of some clarity.

In short, dyes color the wood; pigments cover the wood.

Dyes fall into two categories: natural and synthetic, the latter also known as aniline dyes. Natural dyes date back several centuries, as man discovered roots, plants, and trees which release vibrant colors when soaked in water. Standard ingredients in 18th and early 19th century dye formulas included mandrake root (yellow), as well as wood chips from the logwood tree (black) and Brazilwood trees (red).

Synthetic dyes were invented approximately one hundred and fifty years ago. The largest number of these aniline dyes are derivatives of coal tar and can be dissolved in one of five carriers: water, denatured alcohol, lacquer thinner, mineral spirits, and turpentine.

While a few cabinetmakers clung to their old formulas and continued to dig, grind, boil, and simmer their own natural dyes, by 1900 nearly all furniture factories in the United States had switched to aniline dyes. It appears that all of the major manufacturers of Arts & Crafts furniture utilized natural or aniline dyes either after fuming or in place of fuming.

Evidence of dyes are easy to spot, for dyes are sloppy; ammonia fumes leave no brush marks—even on the bottom. Another need for aniline dyes was explained by Stickley in his instructions for fuming:

"Where any sap wood has been left on, that part will be found unaffected by the fumes. There is apt also to be a slight difference in tone when the piece is not all made from the same log, because some trees contain more tannic acid than others. To meet these conditions it is necessary to make a "touch-up" to even the color. This is done by mixing a brown aniline dye (that will dissolve in alcohol) with German lacquer, commonly known as "banana liquid" [amyl acetate]. The mixture may be thinned with wood alcohol [denatured alcohol] to the right consistency before using. In touching up the lighter portions of the wood the stain may be smoothly blended with the darker tint of the perfectly fumed parts, by rubbing along the line where they join with a piece of dry cheesecloth, closely following the brush. If the stain should dry too fast and the color is left uneven, dampen the cloth very slightly with alcohol."

Gustav Stickley insisted on aniline dyes dissolved in alcohol, for (1) they could be mixed with shellac, his favorite finish, and (2) alcohol does not raise the grain of the wood. Other wood finishers, however, recommended water-soluble dyes, which are easier to work with. Alcohol evaporates more rapidly than water; in the hands of a beginner, alcohol dyes are more apt to leave brush strokes, blotchy patches, and lap marks.

But Stickley stood his ground: "A water stain should never be used, as it raises the grain to such an extent that in sandpapering to make it smooth again, the color is sanded off with the grain, leaving an unevenly stained and very unpleasant surface. The most satisfactory method we know, especially for workers who have had but little experience, is to use a small amount of color carried on in very thin shellac. If the commercial cut shellac is used it should be reduced with alcohol in the proportion of one part of shellac to three of alcohol."

Those who disagreed with Stickley used a different technique to counter the grain raising of water-soluble dyes. In the wood preparation stage, the cabinetmaker would douse the wood with clear water. The loose fibers would absorb the water and swell; then he would sand them off prior to dyeing. When he applied his water-soluble dye, there were no loose fibers to swell, hence there was no grain raising.

Aniline dyes are sold as powders or concentrated liquids. The container will indicate whether the dye is designed to be dissolved in (1) water, (2) denatured alcohol, (3) oil (mineral spirits, turpentine, lacquer thinner), or (4) any of the above.

Water-soluble dyes are the most light resistant of all the aniline dyes. No other dye is easier to mix or apply, nor does any other dye penetrate as quickly or as deeply. The water can raise the grain of the wood, but this can be minimized by the techniques previously explained. For best results, always use distilled water.

Alcohol-soluble dyes don't raise the grain of the wood, but they fade in direct sunlight. This explains why so few examples of Gustav Stickley's green-dyed furniture have survived with their color intact. Alcohol-soluble dyes can be mixed with shellac.

Oil-soluble dyes are seldom used, for they are slow to dissolve in any of the oil-based solvents and do not penetrate as well as water-soluble dyes.

APPLYING ANILINE DYES

1. Sand the wood with #180-grit sandpaper.
2. Moisten the wood with clear water. Allow to dry.
3. Sand off the raised grain with #220-grit sandpaper.
4. Dissolve the dye in the proper carrier until you achieve the desired color.
5. Test the color of the dye on scrap wood.
6. Apply the dye to the wood using a brush or clean cloth. Wipe off any excess and allow overnight to dry.
7. If the grain is rough, sand lightly with #220 sandpaper.
8. If sanding removes any of the color, repeat steps #4 - #6.

CHEMICAL COLORING

The most well-known means of changing the color of wood by chemical action is that of fuming, but other examples of chemical treatments were occasionally employed by furniture makers. As Gustav Stickley wrote in his 1909 *Craftsman Homes*:

"We find that the best effect in both maple and gumwood is obtained by treating the wood with a solution of iron-rust made by throwing iron filings or any small pieces of iron into acid vinegar or a weak solution of acetic acid. After forty-eight hours the solution is drained off and diluted with water until the desired color is obtained. The wood is merely brushed over with this solution, — wetting it thoroughly, — and left to dry. This is a process that requires much experimenting with small pieces of wood before attempting to treat the furniture, as the color does not show until the application is completely dry. By this treatment maple is given a beautiful tone of pale silvery gray and the softwood takes on a soft pale grayish brown...."

The Roycrofters used a similar treatment on oak, keeping "a barrel of soupy water left standing, apparently for years on end, full of rusting nails and other pieces of scrap metal, and wood stain. This bizarre mixture was applied to the furniture by brush and left to stand. "

Chemical coloring is best left to the woodworker with a degree in chemistry. Many of the chemicals, such as dichromate of potassium, ferrous sulphate, or stannous chloride, are dangerous to handle. Also, the reactions depend on the presence of certain chemicals in the wood; many of these chemicals, such as tannin, may have leached out over the years. Finally, since this technique is unpredictable, fine antiques should not be subjected to coloring with obscure and dangerous chemicals.

For more information on chemical coloring, see *Wood Finishing with George Frank* (Sterling Publishing, NY, 1988).

PIGMENTED OIL-BASED STAINS

As Gustav Stickley noted, "Sometimes a home cabinetmaker does not find it practical or desirable to fume the oak. In such a case there are a number of good stains on the market that could be used on oak as well as other woods." His words still ring true, and the most popular stains today are pigmented oil-based stains. Sold under a variety of brand names, they all have much in common:

- most use mineral spirits as a carrier and contain some turpentine, linseed oil, and japan drier
- many contain a small percentage of aniline dyes, but rely heavily on pigments
- most are applied with either a rag or a brush
- after the wood has absorbed much of the stain, the excess is wiped off
- most are compatible with all furniture finishes.

Although aniline dyes represented a major breakthrough for Arts & Crafts furniture makers, the demand still existed for a non-grain-raising, easy-to-use, inexpensive stain for the novice. As a writer for the Popular Mechanics Company book *Mission Furniture: How To Make It* pointed out in 1909, the solution was not perfectly clear:

"What is mission oak stain? There are many on the market, with hardly two alike in tone. The true mission oak stain may be said to show a dull gray, the flakes showing a reddish tint, while the grain of the wood will be almost a dead black. To produce such a stain take 1 lb. of drop black in oil and 1/2 oz. of rose pink in oil, adding a gill of best japan drier, thinning with three half-pints of turpentine. This will make about 1 qt. of stain. Strain it through cheese cloth. Japan colors will give a quicker drying stain than that made with oil colors, and in this case omit the japan and add a little varnish to bind it."

Pigmented oil-based stains are easy to use, but since they do not penetrate any deeper than the top layer of open pores, they have definite drawbacks. First, they can be worn off. Second, they cannot match the true ebony of fuming or dyes without coating the surface with an unattractive layer of pigments. Finally, they are not as effective on the medullary rays of quartersawn oak, for these rays do not have pores to snag the ground pigments.

The final color you can achieve using these stains (also called penetrating oil stains, wiping stains, gels, and other similar names) will be affected by these criteria:

- the color of the pigments and dyes in the stain
- the existing color in the wood
- the amount of stain the wood will accept (new wood absorbs more stain than refinished wood; oak is more porous than maple, etc.)
- the pore structure of the wood
- the length of time the stain remains on the wood
- the amount of stain wiped off the wood.

Like all means of coloring wood, one basic rule should always be followed: experiment on scrap wood, not a fine piece of furniture.

APPLYING A PIGMENTED STAIN

1. Sand the wood with #220-grit sandpaper. Remove the dust.
2. Stir the stain thoroughly to distribute the pigments evenly.
3. Apply a liberal coat of stain with a rag or brush.
4. Wait the determined amount of time to achieve the desired color.
5. Wipe off the excess stain with a clean cloth.
6. Allow 24 hours for the stain to dry.

A second coat of stain can be added the following day, either to deepen the effect or to add a second color. To duplicate the reddish-brown hue, apply a cherry stain first; after it dries follow with dark walnut. The second stain does not penetrate as deeply as the first, which seals most of the pores. This technique is more successful on the open pores of oak than it is on the smaller pores of maple and cherry.

Stains by the same manufacturer can also be mixed together to create custom colors.

Do not make the mistake of letting the pigments dry atop the wood, for they will break loose when the finish flows over them. Always wipe off all of the excess stain before it dries.

PASTE FILLER
67.

While the large pores of oak, ash, and chestnut contribute to the wood's texture and attractiveness, they also pose a problem for us. When new wood emerges from the kiln and old wood from the stripping pan, the natural filler has been destroyed by either the heat or the chemicals. Many finishers hope their first coat of shellac or varnish will replace the lost filler, but that rarely happens on woods with large pores.

As a writer of this period noted, "If a dull finish is desired, apply two coats of stain and two of prepared wax. If a polished surface is wanted, first fill the pores of the wood with any standard filler, which can be purchased at a paint store. After this has dried, rub off any surplus filler, rubbing across the grain of the wood."

Filling the pores is an optional step. If you carefully and gently remove an old finish with a mild solvent and rags, the original filler may remain intact, eliminating the need for this step. If you have to resort to a methylene chloride stripper, coarse steel wool, or a brass bristle brush to dislodge the old finish, you can expect to need paste filler to fill the vacant pores.

Paste filler is available at paint stores as "natural" (tan) or ordered pre-tinted through a woodworkers' supply firm. If you inspect an original finish closely, you will note that the pores are generally filled with black paste filler. If natural paste filler is going to be used on a dark wood, you must first color it using oil-based tints available at paint stores, artist supply shops, and craft stores. Since most paint stores only stock natural paste filler, it is faster to mix your own colors than to order pre-tinted paste filler.

As it is packaged, paste filler is too thick to brush on the wood. I find it easiest to both tint and thin my natural paste filler simultaneously, using a black oil-based tint for color and mineral spirits as a thinner. Add enough mineral spirits to achieve a creamy consistency, then add the tint a drop at a time and blend all three together. I apply the paste filler to the wood using an inexpensive brush with all but one inch of bristles cut off. A stiff brush will enable you to force the paste filler into the pores, where it will begin to dry. Timing is critical, for if you wait too long before wiping off the excess filler, it will harden. If you remove it too soon, you will pull the filler out of the pores.

The paste filler is best applied against the grain of the wood, forcing it into the pores. The same applies to removing the excess filler left on top of the wood. As the filler begins to harden, use a dry, coarse rag to wipe the filler off the wood. Take care not to drag the filler out of the pores. Wait a few minutes longer, giving the filler in the pores additional time to harden. After it does, dampen a clean cloth with mineral spirits and carefully remove any remaining smudges of paste filler on top of the wood. When you are finished, the filler should be in the pores, but not on top of the wood.

The Popular Mechanics guide offered these instructions in 1909: "If the filler is well-stirred and properly applied, one coat ought to be sufficient. If it does not fill the pores satisfactorily, apply another coat when the first has had time to harden. Vandyke brown is used to color the filler, if none but natural color is to be had. On the hardened filler apply a thin coat of shellac. On this apply several coats of wax."

Neatness counts, for any filler left on the wood will have to be sanded off—and the sandpaper may remove some of the color of your dye or stain. To be safe, only work on small sections. Learn on portions which won't be as obvious, saving the tops of tables, sideboards, and servers for last.

APPLYING PASTE FILLER

1. Allow any previous application of stain or dye to dry.
2. Thin the paste filler to a creamy consistency by stirring in small amounts of mineral spirits.
3. Color the filler with an oil-based tint.
4. Use a stiff, short-bristled brush to work the filler into all of the pores.
5. Allow the filler stand until it begins to dry.

> TIP: The first sign that the paste filler is ready to be rubbed off is when it changes color from bright to dull. Test it with your finger tip. If the filler rolls, it is ready. If it smears, have another cup of coffee.

6. Rub off the majority of the surplus filler using a coarse cloth, taking care not to pull the filler out of the pores. Force the filler into any open pores.
7. Allow to stand an additional five to fifteen minutes.
8. Rub off the remaining surplus filler using either a clean dry cloth or, for stubborn spots, a mineral spirits rag.
9. Allow 24 hours for the filler to harden.
10. Sand lightly with #220-grit sandpaper.

ARTS & CRAFTS FINISHES
71.

"What step is taken next will depend upon what
kind of surface is desired. Several coats of polishing
wax may be put on. This is easily done and makes
the most satisfactory finish for mission and craftsman
furniture. It is the easiest to apply. Several coats of
shellac or varnish might be put on instead of wax."
                                    - *Popular Mechanics* (1909)

Arts & Crafts furniture finishes have remained something of a
mystery for collectors. Most professional cabinetmakers and
refinishers now spray nitrocellulose lacquer, which provides
adequate protection, but which falls short of duplicating an
original Arts & Crafts finish. Most amateur woodworkers and
refinishers brush on polyurethane varnish, which also provides more than adequate protection, but which also does not
duplicate an original Arts & Crafts finish. And many custom
furniture makers hand rub an oil finish, such as tung oil, but the
oils don't even come close to looking like the finishes of Gustav
Stickley, Charles Limbert, or the Roycrofters.

The solution to the mystery has long remained within
reach, but few collectors have taken the time to track down
original sources, formulas, and descriptions dating from the
period. If they had, many of the pieces in our collections today
would look more authentic.

SHELLAC

Most Arts & Crafts furniture makers preferred one of three finishes: shellac, varnish, or wax. Of the three, shellac proved to be the most popular, for it was inexpensive, easy to apply, and fast-drying. Although modern polyurethane varnish and nitrocellulose lacquer offer greater resistance to water and alcohol, Arts & Crafts literature does not indicate this was a problem, perhaps because neither alcohol nor house plants were as prevalent in homes as they are today. In addition, nearly every old formula for shellac also calls for a dressing of wax, which strengthens shellac without sacrificing any clarity.

From the Popular Mechanics Company *Mission Furniture: How To Make It* (1909-1912) comes these instructions for a shellac finish:

"For a finish, a coat of paste filler colored so as to give a rich golden brown should be applied first. Allow this to harden, after rubbing and polishing it in the usual manner, then apply a thin coat of shellac. Sand this lightly when hard, and over this apply a coat of orange shellac. Over the shellac put several coats of some good rubbing wax and polish each coat well."

For a slightly different furniture project, the same writer also advised, "Stain the wood any dark color and apply a very thin coat of shellac. Put on wax and you will have a finish that can be renewed at any time by wiping with a little turpentine and rewaxing."

Gustav Stickley also advocated a shellac finish, even going so far as to assume credit for it: "The oak finish which I use has been fumed and finished in a way that preserved the inherent beauties of the wood, with just enough color added to heighten the original effect. This finish, in fact, which I have worked so long to attain, is now recognized as the standard finish for which everyone is striving."

In perhaps the most-often quoted instructions for mixing an Arts & Crafts finish, Stickley recommends that:

"After fuming, sandpapering and touching up a piece of furniture, apply a coat of lacquer, made of one-third white shellac and two-thirds German lacquer. If the fuming process has resulted in a shade dark enough to be satisfactory, this lacquer may be applied clear; if not, it may be darkened by the addition of a small quantity of the stain used in touching up. Care must be taken, however, to carry on the color so lightly that it will not grow muddy under the brush of an inexperienced worker. The danger of this makes it often more advisable to apply two coats of lacquer, each containing a little color. If this is done, sandpaper each coat with very fine sandpaper after it is thoroughly dried and then apply one or more coats of prepared floor wax. These directions, if carefully followed, should give the same effects that characterize the Craftsman furniture."

lacquer - not to be confused with modern nitrocellulose lacquer. In 1912, lacquer loosely referred to any rapidly-drying finish containing shellac as a resin and alcohol as the solvent or carrier; derivations were formerly called lac finish, Rapid-Lac, spirit varnish, lacquer, or shellac.

German lacquer - another name for amyl acetate, a solvent for shellac which is very similar to denatured alcohol.

floor wax - considered the most durable wax available at that time, for it contained carnauba wax, which is now an ingredient in quality furniture waxes.

Although his terminology can be confusing, Gustav was recommending two very thin coats of shellac followed by one or two coats of wax, a standard combination of the era.

Shellac begins as a natural, nontoxic flake which is dissolved in denatured alcohol in various proportions called "cuts." Today, pre-mixed shellac is generally a three-pound cut, wherein three pounds of flakes are dissolved in one gallon of alcohol. Many craftsmen prefer to mix their own shellac, mixing only enough flakes and alcohol as needed, for liquid shellac has a shelf life of less than a year, after which it may not dry properly. For that reasons, always check the date on any can of commercially prepared liquid shellac.

The three-pound cut of shellac is too thick for our needs. Thick shellac tends to have a higher gloss than we desire for

Arts & Crafts furniture. Nearly every original formula calls for *thin* shellac. Refinishers who complain of the high gloss sheen generally are guilty of spraying or brushing on two or more unthinned coats of commercial shellac. This problem existed in 1912, too, for as Stickley pointed out, "shellac, as it is ordinarily cut for commercial purposes, is mixed in the proportion of four pounds to a gallon of alcohol, so that in order to make it thin enough it is necessary to add sufficient alcohol to obtain a mixture of one pound shellac to a gallon of alcohol."

Liquid shellac is available in two forms: white (clear) and orange (amber). In its natural state, shellac has an amber tint, but manufacturers bleach out the natural color to create white shellac. Despite Stickley's preference, I strictly use orange shellac. Since it has not been bleached, it is more durable than white shellac. Orange shellac also looks older than white, for the amber hue helps duplicate natural patina. As a maker of new furniture, Stickley was not as concerned about patina, but as antique collectors, we are.

MIXING SHELLAC

To mix a one-pound cut of shellac:

1. Stir 4 ounces of shellac flakes into one quart of denatured alcohol or, if available, amyl acetate.
2. Let stand for twelve hours, stirring occasionally.
3. Filter through several layers of cheesecloth or paint filter.
4. Bottle and label, including the date and ingredients.

— or —

1. Purchase one quart of liquid shellac (three-pound cut).
2. In a clean, one-gallon container, combine the liquid shellac with two quarts of denatured alcohol or amyl acetate.
3. Filter through several layers of cheesecloth or paint filter.
4. Bottle and label, including the date and ingredients.

APPLYING A NEW SHELLAC FINISH

1. Wait until any applications of stain, dye, or paste filler are completely dry.
2. Vacuum or wipe off any dust from the pores of the wood.
3. Mix or thin your shellac to a one-pound cut.
4. Fold and roll the corners of a 12" square of cheesecloth to make an applicator pad with no exposed edges.
5. Dip the center of the pad into the shellac and rub a thin coat of finish into the wood.
6. Apply the shellac in tight concentric circles to force it into the pores, but complete each board by running your pad the entire length *in the direction of the grain* to remove any swirl marks or excess finish.
7. Although shellac will dry in minutes, wait 8-12 hours for it to completely harden.
8. Sand the shellac lightly with #220 sandpaper or a fine synthetic sanding pad to remove any dried particles.
9. On new or porous wood, repeat steps #2 - #8.
10. Using a cloth, a pad of #0000 steel wool, or a very fine synthetic sanding pad, rub out the hardened finish using a furniture paste wax (see pg. 82 and 86).
11. Buff the paste wax to a hard sheen with cheesecloth.
12. On new or porous woods, repeat steps #10 and #11.

REPAIRING A WORN-OUT SHELLAC FINISH

1. Carefully remove any traces of old wax and polish with a cloth dipped in mineral spirits. Wipe completely dry.
2. Mix or thin your shellac to a one-pound cut.
3. Fold and roll the corners of a 12" square of cheesecloth to make an applicator pad with no exposed edges.

4. Dip the center of the pad into the shellac and rub a thin coat of finish into the wood. Work quickly to avoid dissolving any remaining original finish.
5. Apply the shellac in tight concentric circles to force it into the pores, but complete each board by running your pad the entire length *in the direction of the grain* to remove any swirl marks or excess finish.
6. Although shellac will dry in minutes, wait 8-12 hours for it to completely harden.
7. Apply a coat of high quality furniture paste wax with either a pad of #0000 steel wool or a very fine synthetic sanding pad.
8. Buff to a hard sheen with clean cheesecloth.
9. Allow 24 hours for the wax to harden.

PRESERVING AN ORIGINAL SHELLAC FINISH

1. Carefully remove any traces of old wax and polish with a cloth dipped in mineral spirits. Wipe completely dry.
2. For extremely dry wood, apply a coat of liquid wax.
   2a. If the wood is badly scratched or worn, use dark wax or color the wax with a few drops of a universal tint to match the color of the wood. Buff, then allow to harden.
   2b. If the original finish is rough, use a pad of #0000 steel wool or a very fine synthetic sanding pad as a wax applicator. Buff, then allow to harden.
3. Apply a coat of high quality furniture paste wax with either a cloth, a pad of #0000 steel wool, or a very fine synthetic sanding pad (see pages 82 and 86).
4. Buff to a hard sheen with clean cheesecloth.
5. Allow 24 hours for the wax to harden.

VARNISH

Many writers from this period were divided between shellac and varnish as a finish for oak Arts & Crafts furniture. From the Popular Mechanics Company book *Mission Furniture: How To Make It* (1909-1912) comes the following observation:

"Probably no other finish appeals to so many people as golden oak. Different manufacturers have set standards in their part of the country, but the prevailing idea of golden oak is usually that of a rich reddish brown. Proceed as follows [for] egg shell gloss:

1. One coat of golden oak water stain, diluted with water if a light golden is desired.
2. Allow time to dry, then sandpaper lightly with fine sandpaper. This is to smooth the grain and to bring up the highlights by removing the stain from the wood. Use No. 00 sandpaper and hold it on the fingertips.
3. Apply a second coat of the stain diluted about one-half with water. This will throw the grain into still higher relief and thus produce a still greater contrast. Apply this coat of stain sparingly, using a rag. Should this stain raise the grain, again rub smooth.
4. When this has dried, put on a light coat of thin shellac. Shellac precedes filling that it may prevent the high lights - the solid parts of the wood - from being discolored by the stain in the filler, and thus causing a muddy effect. The shellac being thin does not interfere with the filler's entering the pores of the grain.
5. Sand lightly with fine sandpaper.
6. Fill with paste filler colored to match the stain.
7. Cover this with a coat of orange shellac. This coat of shellac might be omitted, but another coat of varnish must be added.
8. Sandpaper lightly.
9. Apply two or three coats of varnish."

Another writer of the period reveals how shellac and varnish were often used on the same piece, in this example, one stained green:

1. Apply one coat of green Flemish water stain.
2. When this has dried, sandpaper lightly until the raised grain has been removed, and apply another coat of stain diluted one-half with water. Let dry.
3. Sand lightly and apply a very thin coat of shellac.
4. Sand lightly and apply a coat of dark filler, natural filler colored with lampblack, according to the somberness of the finish desired.
5. Upon this put a coat of orange shellac.
6. After this, put on two coats of a good varnish.

Arts & Crafts finishers could select from several different varnishes, including carriage varnish, copal varnish, flexible varnish (recommended for hot air balloons), glass varnish, tar varnish, and mastic varnish. Ironically, in an 1890s book entitled *Lee's Priceless Recipes*, the formula for Furniture Varnish reads as follows:

"Shellac 1-1/2 pounds. Naphtha 1 gallon.
Dissolve and it is ready without filtering."

Varnish, like *lacquer*, could refer to several different formulas.

Oil-based varnishes, however, differ from shellac. *Lee's* formula for copal varnish called for:

"gum copal 8 pounds   linseed oil 2 gallons
sugar of lead 1/2 pound   turpentine 3-1/2 gallons
Boil until stringy."

The copal and the linseed oil provide protective resins which remain behind as a clear film; the lead speeds the drying; and the turpentine serves as the carrier for the ingredients.

MIXING AN ARTS & CRAFTS VARNISH

Since it is nearly impossible to mix an authentic Arts & Crafts varnish, we have to settle for a close substitute. To make slightly more than one quart of varnish, blend together the following:

- three cups of interior, satin oil-based varnish
    (non-polyurethane)
- one cup of turpentine
- one cup of boiled linseed oil

This varnish will be slightly thinner than most modern varnishes and can be applied with either cheesecloth or a brush.

APPLYING A NEW VARNISH FINISH

1. Wait until any stain, dye or paste filler is completely dry.
2. Vacuum or wipe off any dust from the pores of the wood.
3. Mix three parts interior, satin, oil-based varnish (non-polyurethane) with one part turpentine and one part boiled linseed oil.
4. Fold and roll the corners of a 12" square of cheesecloth to make an applicator pad with no exposed edges.
5. Dip the center of the pad into the varnish and rub a thin coat of finish into the wood.
6. Apply the varnish in tight concentric circles to force it into the pores, but complete each board by running your pad the entire length *in the direction of the grain* to remove any swirl marks or excess finish.
7. Wait 24 hours for it to completely harden.
8. Sand the varnish lightly with #220 sandpaper or a fine synthetic sanding pad to remove any dried particles.

9. On new or porous wood, repeat steps #2 - #8.

10. Using a pad of #0000 steel wool, or a very fine synthetic sanding pad, rub out the hardened finish using a high quality furniture paste wax (see pages 82 and 86).

11. Buff the wax to a hard sheen with a clean cheesecloth.

12. On new or porous woods, repeat steps #10 and #11.

REPAIRING A WORN-OUT VARNISH FINISH

1. Carefully remove any traces of old wax and polish with a cloth dipped in mineral spirits. Wipe dry.

2. Mix together the following:
   • one cup interior, satin, oil-based varnish (non-polyurethane)
   • one cup turpentine
   • one-half cup boiled linseed oil.

3. Fold and roll the corners of a 12" square of cheesecloth to make an applicator pad with no exposed edges.

4. Dip the center of the pad into the varnish and rub a thin coat of finish into the wood.

5. Wipe off any excess varnish with a clean cheesecloth.

6. Wait 24 hours for the finish to completely harden.

7. Apply a coat of high quality furniture paste wax with either a pad of #0000 steel wool or a very fine synthetic sanding pad (see pages 82 and 86).

8. Buff to a hard sheen with clean cheesecloth.

9. Allow 24 hours for the wax to harden.

PRESERVING AN ORIGINAL VARNISH FINISH

1. Carefully remove any traces of old wax and polish with a cloth dipped in mineral spirits. Wipe dry.
2. For extremely dry wood, apply a coat of liquid wax.
   2a. If the wood is badly scratched and worn, use dark wax or color the wax with a few drops of a universal tint to match the color of the wood. Buff, then allow to harden.
   2b. If the original finish is rough, use a pad of #0000 steel wool or a very fine synthetic sanding pad as a wax applicator. Buff, then allow to harden.
3. Apply a coat of high quality furniture paste wax with either a cloth, a pad of #0000 steel wool, or a very fine synthetic sanding pad (see pages 82 and 86).
4. Buff to a hard sheen with clean cheesecloth.
5. Allow 24 hours for the wax to harden.

WAX
82.

Woodworkers have known for centuries that wax will protect and preserve wood. Today it is manufactured in liquid or paste form and can be used:

- as a new finish
- in combination with another new finish
- to preserve an old finish
- to rub out a new or an old finish (see page 86).

Beeswax has remained popular for centuries, for it is readily available, inexpensive, and easy to use. But beeswax is neither as strong nor as durable as carnauba wax from South America. Most commercial waxes contain both carnauba and beeswax, for pure carnauba wax is expensive and difficult to spread. The waxes in any formula are thinned with either turpentine or mineral spirits. The strength and the price of commercial waxes are affected by the amount of solvent and the types of wax in the formulas. Proportions of each are often printed on the can.

Liquid wax is a blend of waxes produced by thinning paste wax with mineral spirits or turpentine. Though easier to apply, it provides less protection than paste wax. Liquid wax penetrates deeper into the pores than paste wax, making it useful for preserving extremely dry wood and in maintaining a paste wax finish. Both are important tools in an Arts & Crafts workshop.

Old formulas will occasionally call for floor wax, which previously contained more carnauba wax than did furniture wax. Modern furniture paste wax is considered to be as strong as floor wax from the Arts & Crafts era and should be used in its place.

BLENDING YOUR OWN WAX

Wax is easy to dissolve, blend, or tint. Blocks of beeswax can be purchased from local beekeepers or craft supply stores. Raw carnauba wax is often unavailable in small quantities; you may be limited to working with beeswax and commercially packaged paste and liquid waxes. The two solvents used most often to soften and dissolve wax are turpentine and mineral spirits.

Two formulas for making a beeswax finish appeared in the Popular Mechanics book *Mission Furniture: How To Make It*:

"The most satisfactory finish for mission designs, and the easiest to apply, is wax. It is an old finish that was superseded by varnish. Our ancestors used to make wax polish by "cutting" beeswax with turpentine. Cut up the beeswax and add to it about one-third its volume of turpentine. Heat to the boiling point in a double boiler. Or, melt a quantity of beeswax and to this add an equal volume of turpentine. Care must be taken that the turpentine shall not catch fire."

For those who wish to avoid any risk of fire, the same author offered another formula for liquid wax :

"The process of waxing is simple: Cut some beeswax into fine shreds and place them in a small pot or jar. Pour in a little turpentine, and set aside for half a day, giving it an occasional stir. The wax must be thoroughly dissolved and then more turpentine added until the preparation has the consistency of a thick cream. This can be applied to the wood with a rag and afterward brushed up with a stiff brush."

The dark Arts & Crafts furniture poses a peculiar problem: light-colored wax will often leave the pores a chalky color. A wood finisher from the Arts & Crafts era proposed this practical solution:

"When putting a wax finish on oak or any open-grained wood, the wax will often show white streaks in the pores of the wood. These streaks cannot be removed by rubbing or brushing. Prepared black wax can be purchased, but if you do not have any on hand, ordinary floor wax can be colored black. Melt the floor wax in a can placed in a bucket of hot water. When the wax has become liquid, mix thoroughly into it a little drop black or lampblack [tint]. Allow the wax to cool and harden. This wax will not streak, but will give a smooth, glossy finish."

If you cannot find dark paste or liquid wax, you can tint any wax by following these same directions. When you find cans of commercial dark wax, buy an extra, for many firms have discontinued this line.

PASTE WAX FINISH

1. Make sure any stain, dye, or paste filler is completely dry.
2. (optional) Apply a very thin coat of shellac (see pg. 72).
3. With a soft cloth, rub a thin coat of paste wax into the pores of the wood.
4. Allow the wax to stand five to ten minutes, then rub briskly with clean cheesecloth to polish.
5. Wait 24 hours for the wax to harden.
6. Repeat steps #3-#5.

COMBINATION FINISHES

1. Make sure any stain, dye, or paste filler is completely dry.
2. Apply two coats of shellac or varnish.
3. With a soft cloth, #0000 steel wool, or a very fine synthetic sanding pad, rub on a thin coat of paste wax.

4. Allow the wax to stand five to ten minutes, then rub
 briskly with clean cheesecloth to polish.
5. Wait 24 hours for the wax to harden.
6. On new or porous wood, repeat steps #3-#5.

PRESERVING AN OLD FINISH

1. Carefully remove any trace of old wax and polish with a
 cloth dipped in mineral spirits. Wipe dry.
2. (optional) For extremely dry wood, rub a liberal coat of
 liquid wax into the pores of the wood.
 2a. If the wood is badly scratched and worn, use dark
 wax or color clear wax with a few drops of a universal
 tint (available at paint, artist supply, and craft stores)
 to match the color of the wood.
 2b. If the original finish is rough, use a pad of #0000
 steel wool or a very fine synthetic sanding pad as a
 wax applicator (see page 86).
 2c. Allow to stand five to ten minutes, then rub
 briskly with a clean cheesecloth. Wait 24 hours for
 the wax to harden.
3. Apply a coat of high quality furniture paste wax (if necessary, tinted to cover scratches) with either a cloth, a
 pad of #0000 steel wool, or a very fine synthetic
 sanding pad.
4. Allow the wax to stand five to ten minutes, then rub
 briskly with clean cheesecloth to polish.
5. Allow 24 hours for the wax to harden.
6. Repeat steps #3 - #5 if necessary for additional protection.

RUBBING OUT
86.

Despite our best attempts, no furniture finish ever dries perfectly smooth. Dust, particles of dried finish, loose bristles, and wood fibers inevitably settle in the wet finish, generally just as we turn our backs and walk away. The difference between a professional finish and one applied by an amateur will be noticeable after the final coat: the amateur will consider his work done, while the professional will know that he has one step remaining — rubbing out the finish.

Rubbing out is simply the process of smoothing out the top layer of shellac or varnish. It isn't difficult, but it can be messy, thus many people skip it. Rubbing out doesn't have to be restricted to new finishes; many old finishes grow rough after years of uneven use and can be smoothed out following the same steps. A number of different techniques and materials are available; which one you select matters little. What is important is that you complete the finishing process with a final rubbing out.

PUMICE & ROTTENSTONE

1. Spread a thin layer of mineral oil over the surface.
2. Sprinkle ground pumice over the oil.
3. Rub the pumice-and-oil solution with a blackboard eraser moving in the direction of the grain.
4. Wipe off all of the pumice-and-oil solution.
5. (optional) For a higher gloss, repeat using rottenstone.
5. Apply a coat of paste wax.

LIQUID WAX

1. Spread a thin layer of liquid wax over the surface.
2. Dip a pad of #0000 steel wool or fine synthetic rubbing pad into the liquid wax.
3. Apply slight pressure and rub the lubricated pad in the direction of the grain. Keep the pad wet at all times.
4. Wipe off the excess wax, then allow five to ten minutes for the remaining film of wax to dry.
5. Buff briskly with a pad of clean cheesecloth.
6. Allow twenty-four hours for the wax to harden.
7. (optional) Apply a coat of paste wax for more protection.

PASTE WAX

1. Dip a pad of #0000 steel wool or a fine synthetic rubbing pad into the paste wax.
2. Apply slight pressure and rub the lubricated pad in the direction of the grain. Keep the pad loaded with wax.
3. Lightly wipe off the excess wax, then allow five to ten minutes for the remaining film of wax to dry.
4. Buff briskly with a pad of clean cheesecloth.
5. Allow twenty-four hours for the wax to harden.

WET SANDING

1. Spread a thin layer of mineral oil over the surface.
2. Place a sheet of #600-grit silicon carbide sandpaper (black) on a sanding block and dip it in the oil.
3. Apply slight pressure and rub the wet sandpaper in the direction of the grain.
4. Add oil as necessary to keep the sandpaper lubricated.
5. Wipe off all of the oil.
6. The following day apply a coat of paste wax.

MAINTAINING ARTS & CRAFTS FURNITURE
89.

Pump or aerosol? Rag or feather duster? Oil, polish, or wax?

The questions seem endless, but they are important, and the answers will ease your burden regarding your Arts & Crafts furniture.

First, you must realize one thing: wood is dead. Neither it nor any finish needs to be fed. The only thing "finish feeders" feed are the pockets of the manufacturers.

Second, the major threat to our furniture is the sun. Given enough time, the ultraviolet rays will destroy a finish and bleach out the color of the wood. No clear finish can prevent the ultraviolet rays from reaching the wood. Your only recourses are to (1) block out the sun with curtains or ultraviolet shields on your windows, and (2) avoid leaving furniture in a sunny location for extended periods of time.

Finally, the better the finish, the easier it is to maintain. Before using any piece of furniture, wax it. Dust won't stick to a waxed surface, but will to oil. Once furniture has been waxed, there is no need for weekly applications of dusting sprays, oils, and polishes. Simply wipe off any dust with a cloth dampened with a little water or lemon oil (which is scented mineral oil). If you dislike bottles, opt for a pump over an aerosol can. The propellants in aerosols can damage original finishes. Regardless of the container, always apply the dusting oil to the cloth, not the wood. And never leave any excess oil on the wood, where it will become sticky, and attract dust. The purpose of the dusting oil is to make the dust stick to your cloth; if you leave any oil on the wood, guess what else gets sticky?

Daily Checklist:

- close draperies during peak sunlight hours
- wipe up spills immediately
- protect finishes from the rough edges on pottery; do not use felt pads, for the dyes can penetrate a finish and permanently stain the wood; trim clear plastic lids from coffee cans to fit neatly beneath pottery
- watch for Arts & Crafts tooled leather pads and linens, or design and make your own to use under accessories
- use coasters under glasses and pads under hot pans
- lift, never drag, an object across the wood

Weekly Checklist:

- dust with a damp cloth or one moistened with lemon oil
- use a feather duster on mullions, around hardware, and on prints and paintings
- check under plants for dampness
- take care not to damage the feet and legs of your furniture with a vacuum or mop
- check for veneer chips, which might still be on the floor beneath the piece

Monthly Checklist:

- rearrange items on the tops of tables to prevent bleach 'spots' from the sunlight
- use linens to cover tops exposed to sunlight
- keep as many leaves as possible in your table to minimize the difference caused by bleaching action of the sun; work any extra leaves in the closet into the monthly rotation

Semiannual Checklist:

- apply a beeswax polish to any dry wood or finish, including leather tops, to strengthen the paste wax foundation you applied earlier
- rearrange your furniture and rugs to prevent the sun from bleaching out the color
- document any additions to your collection with photos, videotapes, receipts, and appraisals for your insurance policy

Storage

- never store furniture where the temperature drops below 32 degrees or rises above 100 degrees, or where the relative humidity ventures far from 50%
- check regularly for signs of insect infestation
- cover furniture with lightweight cloth sheets only, for plastic can cause moisture condensation on the finish

What about leather?

Original leather tops and the hard leather used by Arts & Crafts furniture manufacturers on "wraparound" chair seats and footstools should be sealed with paste wax for protection, then maintained according to the directions listed on these two pages for wood. Once the leather is waxed, you are maintaining the wax, not the leather. Like wood, leather is dead. And paste wax is a stronger preservative than leather balm, leather soap, saddle soap, or any similar products, most of which were intended either for shoes or soft leather upholstery, not Stickley chairs and footstools.

SOURCES OF MATERIALS
93.

For many years Arts & Crafts collectors and furniture restorers were stymied in their attempts to find historically appropriate hardware, finishing supplies, and information. Today, however, a growing number of firms and individuals are providing a vast array of materials designed specifically for Arts & Crafts furniture. Many of them are listed on the following pages; new companies are apt to be found in the periodicals dedicated to this movement and also included in this chapter.

Before you need them, write or call the companies listed in this book and request information on their catalogs. Some firms charge a nominal fee for postage and handling. Once you have a catalog in hand, you can generally place an order over the phone. And the best thing about a catalog is that you find things in it you didn't even know were available.

Finally, don't overlook the craftsmen and craftswomen in your own area. Blacksmiths, metalsmiths, upholsterers, refinishers, and cabinetmakers may be able to supply you with the materials you need, from quartersawn oak to a replacement strap hinge on a Stickley sideboard. You can meet a number of them at quality craft shows or see their work on display in craft galleries. Others will be listed in the Yellow Pages or can be recommended by owners of craft supply shops. When you find a great craftsperson, help keep him in business by passing his name along to other collectors. If you don't, he may not be there the next time you need him.

Reproduction Hardware

Chris Efker
Craftsman Hardware
PO Box 161
Marceline, MO 64658
(816) 376-2481

Bruce Szopo
Gustav Stickley Hardware
3860 Ellamae
Oakland, MI 48363
(810) 652-7652

Michael Adams
% Mission Oak Shop
109 Main Street
Putnam, CT 06260
(203) 928-6662

Tony Smith
Buffalo Studios
1925 E. Deere Ave.
Santa Anna, CA 92705
(714) 250-7333

Turner & Seymour
Decorative Upholstery Nails
PO Box 358
Torrington, CT 06790
(203) 489-9214

Woodworkers' Store
21801 Industrial Blvd.
Rogers, MN 55374
(800) 279-4441

B & M Hardware
4399 N. Willow Glen Ct.
Concord, CA 94521
(510) 689-2212

Dyes, Stains, Finishes

H. Behlen & Brothers
Rt. 30N
Amsterdam, NY 12010
(518) 843-1380

Olde Mill Cabinet Shoppe
1660 Camp Betty Washington Rd.
York, PA 17402
(717) 755-8884

Schreiber Paint Co.
(James Day Co. liquid dyes)
15835 East Warren
Detroit, MI 48224
(313) 884-3355

Woodworkers' Store
21801 Industrial Blvd.
Rogers, MN 55374
(800) 279-4441

Wax and Polishes

Roycroft Furniture Polish
Roycroft Shops, Inc.
31 S. Grove St.
East Aurora, NY 14052
(716) 652-3333

Minwax Company
50 Chestnut Ridge Road
Montvale, NJ 07654
(800) 523-9299

Mica

Asheville-Schoonmaker Mica Co.
900 Jefferson Avenue
Box 318
Newport News, VA 23607
804-244-7311

Periodicals

Craftsman Homeowner
31 S. Grove Street
East Aurora, NY 14052
(716) 655-0562

Style 1900   (formerly
*The Quarterly Journal of the
Arts & Crafts Movement)*
9 South Main Street
Lambertville, NJ 08530
(609)397-4104

American Bungalow
123 S. Baldwin Ave.
Sierra Madre, CA 90125
(800) 350-3363

Old House Journal
2 Main Street
Glouster, MA 01930
(508)283-3200

American Woodworker
33 East Minor Street
Emmaus, PA 18098
(215) 967-5171

Fine Woodworking
Taunton Press
63 South Main Street
Newtown, CT 06470

Leather

Dualoy
45 West 34th Street
New York, NY 10001
(212) 736-3360

J.H. Cook & Sons
PO Box 249
Granite Quarry, NC 28072
(704) 279-5568

Books

Mission Furniture: How To Make It
Popular Mechanics Company
Chicago: 1909-1912
reprinted by Dover Publications
New York: 1980

Wood Finishing with George Frank
George Frank
Sterling Publishing, New York:
1988

*The Furniture of Gustav Stickley:
History, Techniques, and Projects*
Joseph Bavaro/Thomas Mossman
Van Nostrand, New York: 1982

The Weekend Refinisher
Bruce Johnson
Ballantine Books
New York: 1989

The Wood Finisher
Bruce Johnson
Ballantine Books
New York: 1993

*Making Authentic Craftsman
Furniture:*
Gustav Stickley
reprinted by Dover Publications
New York: 1986

Chemical Companies

Check your local Yellow Pages.

J.T. Baker Chemical Company
222 Red School Lane
Phillipsburg, NJ 08865

VWR Scientific
3745 Bayshore Blvd.
Brisbane, CA 94005

Books by Bruce Johnson

Bruce Johnson has collected and restored Arts & Crafts furniture since 1970, beginning with his father's Grand Rapids drop-front desk. He has edited and written more than ten books, hundreds of magazine articles, and has been a columnist for *Style: 1900* and *Country Living* magazine for several years. His antique restoration column *Knock On Wood* has appeared every week since 1979 in antiques publications across the country. Johnson hosts the annual Grove Park Inn Arts & Crafts Conference and Antiques Show each February in Asheville, North Carolina, where he, his wife Lydia Jeffries, and two sons, Eric and Blake, live in a 1914 Arts & Crafts home.

The Weekend Refinisher (Ballantine Books, 1989, 300 pgs.) Hailed as "the most popular antique refinishing book to come along in years," The Weekend Refinisher is designed for everyone with good intentions and a few hours time. Johnson provides step-by-step instructions for saving, not just stripping, old finishes, as well as simple instructions for duplicating the look of an antique finish without sacrificing durability. $10

The Wood Finisher (Ballantine Books, 1993, 342 pgs.) Written as the companion volume to the bestselling antique refinishing book of the nineties (The Weekend Refinisher), The Wood Finisher provides easy to follow step-by-step instructions for finishing and refinishing anything made from wood: floors, doors, unfinished furniture, decks, cabinets, moldings, woodwork, trim, windows, and stairways. $12

The Official Identification and Price Guide to the Arts & Crafts Movement, 2nd Edition (House of Collectibles, 1992, 476 pgs.) Still considered "the price guide other price guides should follow," the second edition of one of the best selling books in the Arts & Crafts field has been expanded to include sections on lighting, color woodblock prints, and textiles. New photographs, new prices, new information, and improved binding promise to keep this book at the top of its field. A "must have" book for anyone remotely interested in Arts & Crafts. $13

Fifty Simple Ways To Save Your House (Ballantine Books, 1994, 298 pgs.) From basement to baseboards, attic to eaves, this book will help you catch minor, easy-to-fix problems before they turn into costly headaches. A vital, money-saving book for every homeowner, no matter what age or style your house. $12

To order, send the proper amount plus $2 shipping per book to Bruce Johnson, Box 8773, Asheville, NC 28814.